The Glass of Heaven
The Faith of the Dramatherapist

of related interest

Drama and Healing
The Roots of Drama Therapy
Roger Grainger
ISBN 1 85302 337 X pb

Dramatherapy with Families, Groups and Individuals
Waiting in the Wings
Sue Jennings
ISBN 1 85302 144 X pb
ISBN 1 85302 014 1 hb

Dramatic Approaches to Brief Therapy
Edited by Alida Gersie
ISBN 1 85302 271 3

Dramatherapy
Clinical Studies
Edited by Steve Mitchell
ISBN 1 85302 304 3

Dramatherapy for People with Learning Disabilites
A World of Difference
Anna Chesner
ISBN 1 85302 208 X

Shakespeare as Prompter
The Amending Imagination and the Therapeutic Process
Murray Cox and Alice Theilgaard
Forewords by Adrian Noble and Ismond Rosen
ISBN 1 85302 159 8

The Glass of Heaven
The Faith of the Dramatherapist

Roger Grainger

Jessica Kingsley Publishers
London and Bristol, Pennsylvania

The right of Roger Grainger to be identified as author of this work has been asserted by
him in accordance with the Copyright, Designs and Patents Act 1988.

First published in the United Kingdom in 1995 by
Jessica Kingsley Publishers Ltd
116 Pentonville Road
London N1 9JB, England
and
1900 Frost Road, Suite 101
Bristol, PA 19007, U S A

Copyright © 1995 Roger Grainger

Library of Congress Cataloging in Publication Data
Grainger, Roger
The glass of heaven: the faith of the dramatherapist/ Roger Grainger
p. cm.
Includes bibliographical reference and index
1. Psychodrama. I. Title
RC489. P7G693 1995
616.89' 1523—dc20

British Library Cataloguing in Publication Data
Grainger, Roger
Glass of Heaven: Faith of the Dramatherapist
I. Title
616.891523

ISBN 1-85302-284-5

Printed and Bound in Great Britain by
Athenaeum Press, Gateshead, Tyne and Wear

Contents

Acknowledgement

I would like to thank the following for their help: Edward Bailey, Madeline Anderson-Warren, Alida Gersie, Marina Jenkyns, Doreen Grainger.

For John Casson

A man that looks on glass,
On it may stay his eye;
Or, if he pleaseth, through it pass,
And then the heaven espy.

George Herbert

Spirituality – that which is characterized by an openness towards being, and at the same time by an awareness of what itself is and is not. The two fundamental aspects of the spiritual correspond to these two opennesses: to universal being and to itself.

Concise Theological Dictionary

Introduction

There are many links between psychotherapy and spirituality. Some kinds of psychotherapy are explicitly religious: for example, logotherapy, clinical theology, Jungian analytical psychology. Other approaches to mind-healing make no claim to being religious, or are overtly non-religious: psychoanalysis, rational-emotive theory, gestalt psychotherapy, various applications of behaviourist theory, such as operant conditioning and cognitive therapy. Others, such as client-centred therapy and personal construct psychology, are determinedly neutral, accepting religion as an independent variable to be taken into account as itself and not explained away in terms of something else.

There is a good deal of argument about the scientific status of psychotherapy. How precise can we be about what actually happens in psychological healing? What is the specific healing 'mechanism' at work? Does it in fact help at all to talk in terms of discernible, measurable events, or is the mechanical analogy a misleading one? As Paul Halmos found out, many therapists who start out with a clear plan of underlying psychic process find themselves brought up short by the category of the uncategorisable, the happening that is not recognisably a reaction.

Twenty years ago, the hospital where I worked set up an experimental ward for the special treatment of long-stay institutionalised patients. The ward was run on 'token economy' lines, an adaptation of operant conditioning theory. According to this, behaviour is learned by being immediately reinforced, stamped into a person's (or an animal's) repertoire until it is allowed to 'decay' by withdrawal of the reward. In this case the patients were given tokens which could be exchanged for goods at the ward shop. As soon as anybody behaved sociably or co-operatively he or she received a token. There was no doubt as to the experiment's success. The patients certainly became less withdrawn. However, despite their loyalty to behaviourist explanations, the clinical psychologists remained unconvinced. In setting the experiment up, all sorts of new opportunities for social interaction had been created. Under the new regime, patients who formerly had had as little as possible to do with one another, now found themselves competing and co-operating. Was it token economy that had succeeded, or the opportunity for relationship? Behaviourists, the most mechanistic of psychological theorists, found themselves acknowledging the presence of the imponderable.

Freudians had been acknowledging it, secretly, for some time. Psycho-analysis is a self-explanatory system, claiming to study the mind 'upon foundations similar to those of any other science, such as physics' (Freud, 1949: 65). Ideas like 'love' and 'hate' are perfectly balanced within the system. Love which does not depend on reciprocity, non-ambivalent, other-directed love, does not exist. All the same, it turns out that it is only when this begins to happen between therapist and client that healing takes place. Halmos, writing from the psychoanalytic viewpoint, describes the therapeutic interaction as 'An I–Thou relationship in Buber's sense' (1965: 60). Buber uses this 'primary word of relation' to signify our encounter with otherness understood as a final category: 'In every particular Thou, the primary word addresses the eternal Thou' (1966: 75) This kind of relationship is something that 'cannot be taught in the sense of precepts being given' (1966: 77). In other words, it evades scientific understanding.

William of St Thierry defines 'spiritual' as 'concerning the whole person as influenced by God.' (1085–1148). According to this definition dramatherapy is surely a spiritual approach to psychotherapy, concerned with the person's relation to the source of personhood. In a sense this is true of psychotherapy *per se*, as all such approaches depend on human relationship. Dramatherapy, however, does more. It not only *lives* spirituality in the moment of encounter, it *speaks* spirituality in its mode of communication – but without being verbally explicit or doctrinally precise. It cannot be confined within the limits of a specific organisation of ideas, its own or anyone else's, for it consists of encounter, reflection and renewal. It does not require any explanatory link or intervening variable, either philosophical or literary-critical, to draw attention to its spiritual nature.

CHAPTER 1

The Therapy Itself

The setting is a large room in a community health centre. It is 7.25 pm. A dramatherapy session is due to begin at 7.30 pm. So far only two people have arrived, the therapist (Jean) and Simon, who is about 40 years old, and has recently been made redundant. Jean is doing her best not to appear anxious at the evident lack of support: 'Well, they said they wanted me to come.' At 7.35 the doors of the room open and five more people come in. These are four women, two in their thirties, two ten years older, and a young man: 'We were waiting outside' says the young man. When everybody had taken their coats off Jean suggests that they say what their names are. This is the first session out of a course of ten.

They stand in a circle and say their names: Simon, Bruce, Gwen, Anna, Barbara, Louise, Jean. Nobody seems very sure of themselves.

Jean surveys the group and realises that the ice needs to be broken.

JEAN: Let's play some daft games to get used to one another.

BARBARA: Excuse me, I hope you don't mind, but I just came along
           with Louise. I'd like to stay on the sidelines if you don't
           mind.

JEAN: I'll tell you what. This bit's only about names. If you get to
           something you don't like, you can drop out. OK?

Barbara grins sheepishly and nods. Jean's name game consists in saying one's own name and then saying the name of the person to the left or right of oneself, who then has to do the same thing. Nobody knows which way this will go, and sometimes it just goes backwards and forwards. After a bit people begin to laugh at the battles arising from this. Bruce mentions another game that he likes: 'Grandmother's Footsteps'. This consists of creeping up and trying to steal a bunch of keys from in front of a blindfolded person. The group plays this for a while, until everyone – including Barbara – has been blindfolded. Everybody is a good deal more relaxed by now.

JEAN: 'What's it all about, d'you think?'

SIMON: 'Fooling about, if you ask me.'

ANNA: 'Getting people to relax?'

JEAN: 'Well, it's certainly about people. This first session's about getting to know one another.'

She asks the group to divide up into pairs, choosing someone that they don't know as a partner. (Barbara and Louise are allowed to be partners.) The partners stand facing each other, with the palms of their hands almost touching ('so you can feel the warmth arising from the other person's palm'). One person moves her or his hands while the other follows, as if they were reflections in a mirror. First one leads, then the other. Slowly, quickly, slowly again. Louise and Barbara turn out to be very skilful, and move round the room mirroring each other. Keeping the same partners, people play a game in which one of them turns away, while the other changes his or her appearance very slightly: 'What's different about me?'

JEAN: 'See if you can remember something about the other person so well, that you can say it as if it were you.'

Partners tell each other the history of the clothes they are wearing. Having done this, they report to the rest in the group in the following way:

GWEN: 'I am Bruce [*her partner*] and I bought these shoes from my twin brother, etc…'

People find this role-reversal rather hard at first, and keep slipping into the third person ('I am Louise, and she bought her jumper', etc…). Once they have got used to doing it, most of the group find it fun. Even Barbara makes no move to back out. Jean gives everyone a subject to discuss: should members of the British royal family make use of the state school system? She has chosen something which people are likely to disagree about. After a few minutes, Bruce and Gwen complain they have nothing more to say to each other on this subject – can they talk about something else? Jean says, by all means, and they go on talking. After about ten minutes the group re-assembles, in order for the pairs to report back. The same role-reversal technique is used. Bruce and Gwen make everyone laugh because of the exaggerated account they give of their (i.e. the other's) views. Jean points out that swapping identities can make self-expression easier sometimes. It always makes understanding the other easier. She goes on to say that today's session had not been very typical of dramatherapy, because there had been so much discussion. Dramatherapists liked to show things rather than talk about them. This was the first session, however, and the main thing was to get to know one another. Seeing they had been exchanging identity, they'd better become themselves again! She suggested that everyone turned to the person on her or his right and said goodbye, calling them by their real name and shaking their hands.

Dramatherapy is one of a group of arts or creative therapies which also includes art, music, and dance/movement therapy. Art and music therapy have been recognised parts of the National Health Service for some years; dramatherapy has only recently been granted this kind of 'official' status. At the time of writing five post-graduate or post-experiential courses have their qualifications validated by the Department of Education and Science, which means that, to all intents and purposes, everyone who is a full member of the Association for Dramatherapists can apply for one of the new jobs that appear now and again in the press, which announces a vacancy for a full or part-time dramatherapist in an NHS hospital or clinic. Many dramatherapists work independently, however, preferring a less institutional approach. In a relatively short time, dramatherapy has established itself inside and outside the state system as an emergent profession, commanding a good deal of respect in places where the medical approach to healing was never previously challenged.

This could not have happened without an immense amount of work carried out over the last 30 years by the founders of dramatherapy. For many in Great Britain and some other countries, Sue Jennings, more than any other single figure, typifies dramatherapy, although she herself is the first to admit her debt to a great many other people from a good many backgrounds — actors, psychotherapists, nurses, social workers, clinical psychologists, psychiatrists, puppeteers, priests, theatre directors, community workers, etc. They were all people who themselves had experienced the spiritually liberating, psychologically healing power of theatre, and were determined to explore ways of making it clinically available. Unfortunately what was so very clear to them, was far from obvious to others. The first dramatherapists were united in their determination to overcome ignorance, misunderstanding and plain prejudice on the part of the therapeutic establishment. Scientific medicine requires replicable effect and logical connections — conclusions drawn according to its own kind of logic, that is. The sense made by the procedures and explanations of dramatherapy does not always accord with the parsimonious reasoning required by positivism. Health workers trained to be doctors, nurses and psychologists found an art-based therapy hard to take seriously – after all, art and science are usually regarded as opposites.

When, after long months of negotiation, and even longer ones taken up demonstrating its real contribution to healing, dramatherapy finally achieved the status of professional recognition within the NHS, dramatherapists were relieved to have achieved the 'official' identity that they had aimed at. They were eager to point out, however, that their work was valuable whether official or not; and that only they could really say what constituted good dramatherapy practice, which the profession was eager to recognise and promote through the agencies for training and supervision set up by the British Association for Dramatherapists. In fact, dramatherapy gives more to the Health Service than it gains from it. Its gains are respectability and prestige, and the opportunity to work alongside other approaches within the areas traditionally associated with psychotherapy. What it provides, however, is scope for experiment in personhood, experience in relationships, and the expression of value, meaning and authority in human life, all of them healing events.

This is not to say that dramatherapy is unconnected with other approaches to healing. Its ancestry is both complex and distinguished. Broadly speaking, its background is in therapeutic drama, psychology and anthropology. The connection between drama and psychological healing has been well established since Aristotle's time. This connection is not based primarily on medical knowledge, as the areas of human experience concerned are ones that have not always been satisfactorily accounted for by medicine. Traditional explanations of drama's well-documented ability to 're-organise' awareness are philosophical, psychological and aesthetic. Theory based on dramatic experience must take account of intangibles. The connection between the theory of drama and the practice and theory of dramatherapy is an on-going one. Notable contributors in this sphere are Bruce Wilshire (1982), Robert Landy (1986) and T.J. Scheff (1980).

Jennings describes the difficulties that dramatherapy encountered as a non-medical approach to healing: 'It has taken work over the last 25 years for dramatherapists to reach the point where they can articulate their philosophy without needing other disciplines to authenticate it.' She describes some of the theoretical requirements for successful practice:

> A working understanding of Aristotle, Plato, Stanislavski, Brecht, Grotowski, Wilshire, Viktor Turner, Boal and Peter Brook, together with an in-depth knowledge of major plays from ancient Greece and Shakespeare, through to Beckett, Sartre and Pinter, and on to the immediate present with Caryl Churchill and David Hare; a thorough

grounding in movement, improvisation, scripts, performance, masks, myth; as actor, director, choreographer. This is the foundation of being a dramatherapist. (1990: 9–10)

(One should not, however, limit oneself to British writers!)

The emergence of psychology as a 'scientific' discipline actually strengthened the connection between drama and healing. Dynamic psychology, social psychology and cognitive approaches all developed psychotherapies which implied that awareness of the importance of hypothetical reality on which drama depends – object relations, symbolic interactionism, Kelleian fixed role therapy.[1] The best known (and documented) example of dramatic psychotherapy is, of course, psychodrama, the invention of Freud's ex-disciple, Moreno (1946: 7; 1959). Modern dramatherapy makes use of a range of insights and techniques of psychodrama, but is more genuinely dramatic in its use of metaphor and in preferring fictional plots to straight autobiography. In fact, as we shall see, the distinctive characteristic of dramatherapy is the obliqueness of its approach; it concentrates on mirroring our condition, not directly reproducing it. Dramatherapists are able to work alongside doctors very much as clinical psychologists do. Like psychologists, they believe change takes place through learning, and results in still more learning. The kind of thing that is learned, and the way it is learned, distinguishes them from psychoanalysts and behaviourists.

A third source of modern dramatherapy is anthropology. Cultures which have retained more of their traditional forms of corporate self-expression provide models for self-discovery by means of group experience. Anthropological awareness opens the door to ways of perceiving the world that have been forgotten, neglected or ignored. The discoveries made through metaphor are here developed and explored, personal insight finding expression in corporate awareness. This source of dramatherapeutic material has been explored by Sue Jennings, whose experiences as an anthropologist have had considerable influence in the development of dramatherapy (1983, 1990, 1995). Alida Gersie has made exhaustive studies of folk-lore (1990). I myself

---

1 *Object relations theory* is an explanation of human relationship in terms of the development of infantile fantasy to take account of the mother as a separate person (Winnicott, 1971). *Symbolic interactionism* refers to our use of symbols to 'see ourselves as other see us', upon which human communication depends (Mead, 1967). *Fixed role therapy* is a clinical approach associated with personal construct psychology by means of which individuals devise and practise a new way of seeing themselves, and consequently presenting themselves to the world (Kelly, 1955)

have been concerned with ways in which ritual is able to translate idea into event, a process fundamental to dramatherapy (Grainger, 1990).

Finally, dramatherapists are involving themselves increasingly in research. Because of the nature of the subject matter, problems of validation are particularly salient. (The difficulty is to be sure what it is that one is being experimentally vigorous about!) Nevertheless, a good deal of medical opinion acknowledges the vital importance of factors within interpersonal situations that defy scientific identification. Dramatherapy's involvement in 'new paradigm' (Reason and Rowan, 1981) research investigations aims at achieving compatibility with the procedures adopted by medical research.

What, then, is dramatherapy? In the first place, it is not psychodrama. *Psychodrama*, as devised and developed by Jacob Moreno, is the realisation in dramatic form of current interpersonal situations. Set in the present it refers to what is actually going on in a particular person's life; the person, that is, who is the protagonist of the drama and becomes the object of the focused empathic imagination of everyone taking part in the action. Dramatherapy also uses drama, but in a less direct way. Dramatherapy's approach is less intentionally directed upon a particular individual who has been identified beforehand. If psychodrama is a powerful frontal assault, dramatherapy uses an oblique approach in which the purpose of the session emerges as the events unfold. Nobody knows to begin with what direction events will take. To this extent, dramatherapy resembles improvised drama. Similarly, its subject matter is fictional rather than autobiographical, personal material being dealt with at one remove; we identify with the characters in the play.

Dramatherapists work in many ways, according to circumstances varying the directness of their approach and the degree of their control over the action. The following is a group model. The approach can be used with smaller groups, and even with individual clients:

> Between 8 and 20 individuals are under the direction of a therapist. To begin with, everybody stands in a circle, and exercises are performed and games played to establish the identity of those present *as a group*, and to help people to feel less self-conscious. (This part of the proceedings usually begins in an atmosphere of wariness, even suspicion, with nobody knowing what is going to happen next, and ends with a certain amount of hilarity.) At this point people may be invited to reveal how they are feeling, what sort of a week they have had, what they felt like when they got up this morning, etc. They do this by demonstrating it in one way or another, but not actually describing it in words – drawing or painting pictures, creating 'living

sculptures' out of one another's bodies, miming sequences of actions, etc.

Out of this it may happen that a theme arises that expresses the feeling of the group. The therapist helps them identify possibilities, and asks them to portray these, working as a group. An idea such as 'the struggle to care for others without going under as an individual', or 'pressing onwards to a time when all of this will make sense', or simply 'searching' may emerge. Perhaps members will recognise themselves and their own struggle in the dramas that ensue. Perhaps not this time. Nobody is forced to reveal anything, and if someone does, they are held within the strength and comfort of the group. The session may end by resumption of the circle; the things that have been happening are related to on-going events 'outside'. People 'come down to earth', say goodbye, and leave.

This is intended to be an example of a more or less typical dramatherapy session. At least the shape, with two outer sections enclosing a more spontaneous and free central part, is invariable. Shape is perhaps the most important characteristic of this form of therapy. The creative dynamic involves experimenting with ritual and spontaneity in order to discover ways of containing the chaos which is at the heart of change – which allows real change to happen. Conforming to Van Gennep's (1960) classical model of a rite of passage, a dramatherapy session has pre-liminal, liminal and post-liminal phases. It is this three-fold configuration that communicates a sense of completeness, of something real having happened, a genuine event which has changed the nature of reality as real events must inevitably do in order to be real.

Dramatherapy uses shape to transmit a message about life, not simply *a* life. It has been defined in several ways, but only with limited success. Dorothy Langley's definition is brief and to the point, but leaves some important things unsaid: dramatherapy is 'the use of drama as a therapeutic tool'. She goes on to point out that 'drama is not, as in theatre, an acquired skill which people can or cannot do, but a medium in which each person can participate at his own level' (1983: 14). Sue Jennings is even more succinct: 'Dramatherapy is the intentional use of drama in order to effect healing and bring about change' (1983: 3). When dramatherapists try to explain precisely how this happens, however, problems can arise: 'The temptation is to try and find an all-embracing definition of dramatherapy and a clear understanding of what it is and also what it is not. Perhaps in other subjects this may be possible, however drama in itself does not allow us to be so finite' (1987:

xiv). There has always been, and perhaps always will be, a tension between the tendency which regards drama as one of several ways of implementing a particular kind of psychotherapy, and the one which recognises a unique kind of therapy which is implicit in drama alone. According to Gordon Langley, drama:

> permits the review of established strategies of living and experimentation with new ones. It expands the individual's repertoire of interpersonal skills, and, where necessary, allows him to examine more closely the grammar of his interactions with other people, making, in the end, for a more flexible performance, whether the change be towards behaviour that is more controlled or more expressive. (Langley, 1983: 172)

Dr Langley's definition is an extension of Peter Slade's: 'It is drama, the doing of life, by which man may experience many situations, thus moving towards maturity, and assume various roles until he discovers more nearly the best of who or what he really is' (1981: 92). Dramatherapy provides a life-like setting in which things can be consciously learned, in order to be systematically reproduced, things about the self and other people which are essential to the business of carrying on social life. This is one model of the way dramatherapy works. It could be called the 'school' model, because it depends on instrumental processes of teaching and learning. It should be pointed out that there is good evidence to suggest that it does work like this (Grainger, 1990).

This is not the only way in which it works, however. Dramatherapists regard the dramatic event as much more than a medium. This is more than a suitable place for something to happen in: it is itself the thing that happens. Drama is understood as being creative rather than merely reproductive. As such it has immense therapeutic potential for those who believe that creative expression of feelings and attitudes is a pathway to the achievement of psychological health and insight (Johnson, 1981: 13). The drama in dramatherapy is precisely what the treatment consists of, what it is about. Casson says, 'It is axiomatic to dramatherapy that the drama is not just a technique but is in itself therapeutic' (1989). Dramatherapy joins other 'creative' therapies – art, music and dance – in the realm of the aesthetic, where healing takes place spontaneously because the setting itself is somehow therapeutic.

Healing that does not limit itself to scientific explanation is open to other kinds of interpretation; and several who have theorised on the subject regard drama as a locus of spirit. Indeed, some have seen dramatherapy as first and foremost 'a spiritual search' (Grainger, 1990), founding their arguments, not on its dialectic usefulness but on the mysterious nature of the creative process enshrined in it, 'The struggle to bring into existence new kinds of being that give harmony and integration' (May, 1975: 140). Dramatherapy's artistic form reproduces its own balance and harmony within the experience of those who take part in it, a process which stretches the categories of behaviouristic psychology somewhat. Some dramatherapists share a passionate need to find meaning, not simply facts. They look for 'unity behind the discontinuities of the world of objects and stimuli, and to discover some sort of significance which helps them transcend the transitoriness of actual experience' (Gordon, 1983: 3). In other words, they are made conscious of eternity within the time span imposed by the drama.

Because of its spiritual implications, we might call this the 'tabernacle' (or 'tent of meeting') model of dramatherapy as opposed to the 'school' one. The models are not mutually contradictory; both may be, and are, frequently used by the same therapist, or even within the same session. To concentrate on the second entirely to the exclusion of the first would be to miss useful opportunities for the sharing of understanding, and instruction in how to enjoy being human; apart from which it is very unlikely that any session could take place without some kind of conscious learning. To concentrate on the first model and ignore the second, however, may be to miss the point completely – there are other ways of teaching and being taught, but no other ways of experiencing drama than drama itself. In fact there is no need to choose, as the art-form combines cognition and intuition, analysis and inspiration, in its own distinctive way: 'The unique potential of dramatherapy is that it can, in one coherent process, unite the intuitive/expressive instinct of the artist, the precise and controlled skill of the therapist, and the ritualistic and spiritual yearning of the religious man' (Koltai, 1981: 210). 'Tabernacle' and 'school' are important aspects of dramatherapy. 'Tabernacle' is the more important of the two. In later chapters, I shall be examining some of the ways in which the spiritual identity of dramatherapy continues to be explained and explored, including, in Appendix II, an investigation of the attitudes of dramatherapists themselves. Before doing this, it is necessary to take an introductory look at some of the basic characteristics of dramatherapy as a way of helping disturbed and alienated individuals towards spiritual serenity and psychological health.

As I said, the distinctive characteristic of dramatherapy is the obliqueness of its approach. That is why it is called dramatherapy. In drama we are both distanced from, and involved in, other people's experience of living; distanced by an awareness that things are not really what they seem, and that a particular piece of social interaction has been 'set up' for us to examine in detail from an (apparently) detached point of view; involved because the means used to set this up have a focusing effect on our awareness which somehow involves us in the action, and helps us to identify what is going on. Because it is a form of theatre, dramatherapy allows us to look at other people 'through their own eyes' rather than 'from the outside'. At the same time, the metaphorical nature of the proceedings, its use of aesthetic distance, prevents the intimacy of role-reversal from being felt as an invasion of privacy. The use of fiction concentrates imagination in a way that permits safe involvement.

Thus dramatherapy aims at combining safety and danger in ways that encourage psychological growth. Within the group, an atmosphere of personal security is fostered in order to permit freedom of self-disclosure, whilst the dramatic process itself allows the 'loosening' and 'tightening' of thought structures (mental constructs) necessary for arriving at new ways of looking at oneself and other people. (An analytically orientated therapist would point to the ability of art to put us in touch with sub-conscious truths demanding expression. The effect of dramatherapy is not only cathartic, but also constructive.)

Dramatherapy sessions are not necessarily time-limited. Each session is self-contained, but sessions may follow on from each other. The number and length of sessions may be decided upon beforehand in accordance with a verbal contract between the therapist and the group members; again, this depends on the particular circumstances. These are typical arrangements; the kind of group involved, the length of sessions, the extent of the whole course, the possibility of further courses, may be negotiable. Like drama itself, dramatherapy takes many forms, from simple personal interchanges to actual plays, of various degrees of formality. It is the dramatic *principle* which is being explored and developed here: a way of looking at, and participating in, life which 'speaks the language' of human relationships, the language of human loving.

To this end, many things happen within the dramatic framework: there is practice in movement and speech, paying attention to people as people rather than objects to be avoided or included, finding new ways of dividing the world up and relating to its parts; there is systematic endorsement for those whose interpretation of themselves and other people lacks a recognisable structure (dramatherapy has been shown to be useful in treating thought-disorder); there is a release from a world that is *too* structured, too demanding, in the exploration of possibilities and the extension of one's repertoire of ways of being in the world.

In the final third of each session, the need to 'come back to earth' again and resume ordinary life is faced within the context of ideas and feelings experienced during the main part of the session. This is called *de-roling*. Just as important, however, is the function of *re-roling*, as the group member's experience of him/herself is rarely the same when he/she leaves the session as it was when he/she first arrived.

To sum up: dramatherapy has a healing effect because it embodies a view of life that does not approach meaning head-on, but lives imaginatively and creatively *with* meanings until human truth is ready to emerge. In particular, dramatherapy experiments with structures for communication (symbols) in order to discover new ones which are able to deliver us from our bondage to ideas and attitudes that have outworn their usefulness. It is not an example of spiritual psychotherapy in the sense of requiring assent to a system of religious beliefs or depending on a state of mind which is explicitly religious. Instead, it is *implicitly* spiritual because of its medium, the acted story which has transpersonal significance, and its subject-matter which characteristically concerns an experience in which the self is transcended. What is expressed here by movement and gesture, in the juxtaposition of objects and people, the silent picturing of relationship and the tumultuous din that forbids thought, is a message about realities that go beyond words – a message that says 'you cannot possibly accommodate me, yet I am here *for* you'. In so far as dramatherapy achieves the pitch of concentration typified in ritual it becomes an authentically spiritual happening.

When this happens, it is not by mistake; as a principle, dramatherapy values non-verbal communication in the attempt to achieve greater expressiveness. In a dramatherapy session, people concentrate on finding ways of expressing themselves that are as direct and explicit as may be. Instead of hiding behind spoken or written language – where phrases have become tarnished by so much easy glibness, so much apparent frankness – they try to discover new images, new ways of being in the ritual space, brought into intimacy by the symbol which divides and unites, expressing intention so vividly and dramatically. 'Don't tell me, show me', says the leader, 'make it live for me.' More can be lived than can possibly be told. As in every genuine social ritual, the intensity of the encounter pre-empts cognition and renders it a secondary phenomenon making encounter the paramount reality.

CHAPTER 2

Drama and the Language of Love

Love and What It Isn't

First of all, I must make it quite clear what I mean by love. According to the *Oxford English Dictionary*, it is 'warm affection, attachment, likeness, or fondness... of, for, to, or towards a person, for or to a thing'. The love I am considering here is concerned with other persons. It is unavoidably social, even centrifugal. It is more a love *to* or *towards* than *of* or *for* the other, and this is what keeps it social. This is not the erotic love which fulfils an instinctual urge for possession or containment and is involved in psycho-physical dependencies. This love does not proceed from libidinal satisfaction. It is the love which bestows and receives gifts. The satisfaction it receives is that of giving in order to create relationship; it receives as part of the gift. This love of exchanging being is sociogenic. It is experienced as originating elsewhere, because it moves backwards and forwards among people, forging invisible ties everywhere it touches. Christian tradition calls it agapé and distinguishes it from eros, whose aim is to enlarge the self by direct enjoyment of the other. Always and everywhere it is agapé that heals.

Drama communicates by means of our awareness of having some kind of personal relationship with the people in the play who have been brought to life by the action of shared imagination as this becomes living flesh in the theatrical event. In the play we recognise our fellow human beings and reach out to them in love. The play is a place where we are healed by love: a place where we can find out how love really works, perhaps even what it really *is*.

When we say that we love someone, we mean that the image of that person in our minds is highly charged with affectionate, constructive and generous feelings. In itself love is a pleasant experience, although it may involve us in a good deal of sorrow. It is characteristically experienced as one of a group of feelings running concurrently: when we love, we are reminded to do other things as well – just as other things remind us of the love we had temporarily forgotten. Psychologically speaking 'reminded' is the wrong word, as these associated feelings and ideas trigger one another off at a level below that of conscious thought. Psychoanalysis claims that feelings which are normally held to be opposites are closely identified at the unconscious level. At this level, love goes hand in hand with hate. Both are under the authority of the controlling pleasure principle which exerts the primary pressure within every individual's psychic economy, and both may contribute to that principle's satisfaction (which is why a woman may murder a man with whom she is 'violently in love'). Classical psychoanalysis maintains that all human loving is affected by the power of this principle, and that love itself is invariably ambivalent towards its object.

Freud is concerned here with love as the organism's delight in someone else for the pleasure that the other person provides. It is love that we *feel*, rather than that we show. In this it is reminiscent of classical Greek 'eros' – basically sexual love, but spiritualised by both Plato and Aristotle. In both senses it denotes a love that is called forth by the inherent worth of its object, which it desires to possess and enjoy. It seeks its object solely for its own satisfaction and self-enhancement. Again it is an experience that we have, an urge that we feel. In this it is quite different from love that is specifically religious, and concentrates on divine, self-revelation – the love that God offers. The New Testament agapé is definitely divine love, even though it refers to the love among fellow Christians; the love with which we are to love one another is actually the divine love itself poured into us and overflowing into the lives of others – an extension of God's love for us (Romans, 5: 5, 6; cf. also John, 13: 34–35: 'I give you a new commandment: love one another: just as I have loved you, you also must love one another. By this love you have for one another, everyone will know you are my disciples').

Christian ideas of love reflect Jewish ones particularly in the stress laid upon practical evidence of love: according to Maimonides, 'There are eight degrees in the giving of charity, each one higher than that which follows it. The highest degree, exceeded by none, is giving a gift or a loan or taking one as a partner or finding him employment by which he can be self supporting' (Hertzberg, 1968: 106). The divine love described in Psalm 23 is to be reproduced in ordinary daily living. The Koran interprets love in terms of compassion shown towards others. Allah is addressed throughout as 'the Merciful, the Compassionate', expressing his divine nature in the care he shows to his creation:

> Did He not find thee an orphan and shelter thee?
> Did He not find thee erring and guide thee?
> Did He not find thee needy and suffice thee? (XCIII)

and the way in which he forgives sins: 'God is All-forgiving, All-compassionate' (II). Among his names is that of *Al Ghaffar*: 'The Forgiving One'. As in Jewish and Christian teaching, Allah's forgiveness involves the willingness of all who benefit from it to show forgiving love to others: 'Woe to those who display and refuse charity' (CVII). This mirroring of natures between a personal god and his universe of people associated within, and constituted by, a relationship of love binds the great religions of the world together. At this profound level, that of the centrality of personal love, believers find little to disagree about. Even Hinduism belongs within the fold:

> The great divide between Hinduism and Buddhism seems to be... between the point of view according to which the love of a personal God is the very crown of the experience of liberation from bondage to which man has been subject, and a point of view where the love of God is acclaimed only as a preparation, even if a necessary one, for realising the goal of such liberation. (Sivaraman, 1974: 3)

Although personal love may not be the ultimate value for Buddhism, as it is for Judaism, Christianity, Islam and Hinduism, it represents a vital stage in the achievement of perfection: 'Great compassion and a great pitying heart is called Buddha-nature. A Bodhisattva should think: I wish to suffer the sufferings of hell for the sake of all beings, so as to make them come to the realisation of Enlightenment' (Masson, 1978: 230).

The love described by the great religions is a relationship, not an instinct. In other words, these faiths describe something taking place between or among people, rather than an interior disposition either learned or characteristic of the species *as* a species. Love is not a way in which we satisfy an urge or indulge a habit. We have to admit that this way of looking at it – love as an event rather than psychological symptom – seems more in accord with our experience. At the most immediate level of response, we find it hard to entertain the idea of love without imagining the experience of loving and so introducing the other into our awareness, introducing them as themselves and not as one of our own ideas – as quite specifically *not* us. Indeed that is the nature of the exercise, the quality of the particular experience. Love is like that; it cannot be otherwise and remain itself. To make it mean an instinct rather than a relation is to reduce it out of all recognition.

This was the conclusion reached by Ian Suttie, who pioneered the object relations school of psychoanalysis and whose work has been massively supported by John Bowlby's research into the effects of maternal deprivation (1981). According to Suttie, the human mind is motivated from the start by the need for responsive companionship. As soon as an infant has developed to the point that it is aware of anything at all – before it is actually born, that is – she or he is involved in relationship. 'We can reject once and for all', says Suttie,

> the notion of the infant mind being a bundle of co-operating or competing instincts, and suppose that it is dominated from the beginning by the need to retain the mother – a need which, if thwarted, must produce the utmost extreme of terror and rage... The need for a mother is primarily presented to the child mind as a need for company and as a discomfort in isolation (1988: 15, 16).

At this primal level acceptance and responsiveness are all. We are not isolated organisms driven by the need to reduce instinctual pressures, but potential people, functioning as ourselves precisely as we function with regard to others. Freud's claim that love originates as narcissism, developing from the infant's love of him or herself is strongly rejected – 'I regard love as social rather than sexual in its biological function, as derived from the self-preservative instincts not the genital appetite, and as seeking any state of responsiveness as its goal' (Suttie, 1988: 36). Anxiety is the fear of losing contact with the other, rather than of being deprived of instinctual gratification. The amazing thing is that the latter is secondary to the former: it is the other person that we want, and we want them from the beginning.

We want them for giving as well as taking. For knowing they are there by their knowing we are here; for responding to us. In the words of J. A. Hadfield, 'The companionship (love) upon which the sense of security depends is reciprocal' (in Suttie 1988: xlvii). We categorise it as love specifically because of its reciprocity:

> The baby not only starts life with a benevolent attitude, but the Need-to-Give continues as a dominant motive through life. The mother–child relationship however (to the child's mind) is a true, 'balanced' symbiosis; and *the need to give is as vital as the need to get*. The feeling that our gifts (love) are not acceptable is as intolerable as the feeling that other's gifts are no longer obtainable. (Suttie, 1988: 53, italics original)

'Religion', says Suttie, aims 'to reconstitute the tender relationship with the human environment which is lost in early childhood.' It forms one of the ways in which we recapture the sense of social security we lose by graduating into the discipline of childhood from the unconditional love of infancy (1988: 3). Teaching about a merciful and loving God is a source of spiritual comfort which has a great effect upon our emotional maturation. We should perhaps note that, according to Suttie, it is the maternal aspect of God that has this life-giving effect on us: also, that his approach is diametrically opposed to Freud, who regards all religion as founded solely upon fear of the father.

Certainly our maturity as persons depends on the experiences of mutuality recognised and described by the object relations psychologists. From their first moments and hours babies are stimulated by the attention of their mothers or those caring for them. The purpose of this ceaseless attention is to develop reciprocity, to open the world to a new individual in the context of a love that is flexible, imaginative, empathic, persistent, devoted, indestructible. This is the only way that the world can be opened – not from inside a person, but between people. Certainly, fathers are not excluded from this basic person building; however, the fact remains that at this stage it implies the mother, and male parents are conscious of taking on someone else's role when they are drafted for service in this area.

And yet, as Suttie points out, we cross this boundary every time we think of love as it is in itself, the essential being of love, free from any kind of selfishness. This kind of love is essentially maternal, and yet in religious thought we associate it with a range of male deities. It seems that in its origin, love is too powerful and primal to be tied down to what we do with it, how we express or embody it. It bursts through our categories, leading and following, giving and receiving, involving and liberating, reassuring and teasing, testing and validating. Love echoes our being and toughens our identity. It is a kind of realism of the spirit, giving depth and purpose and meaning to life, making awareness complete. What is seen in love is perceived multi-dimensionally. As a thought, an idea, it always lacks substance; instinctual drives appear to be much more tangible and worthy of scientific interest; but the experience of love as the joy of giving and receiving is far too convincing a fact to be explained away as a diversion of selfishness prompted by fear.

Quite early on in the history of psychoanalysis, Ferenzi came to the conclusion that the healing factor in therapy was love rather than science. 'It is the physician's love that heals the patient' (1950). He was not alone in thinking this. Paul Halmos's book, *The Faith of the Counsellors* (1965), examines the opinions of psychoanalysts who have come to the same conclusion although subscribing to a philosophy which explicitly denies the existence of love in any unselfish sense. Despite the difference in world-view between scientist and theologian, there is no doubt that the 'personal love' of religious belief and the healing love of inter-personal psychotherapy are the same thing. The persons are different but the event is the same; by which I mean that some of those involved may be categorised as human, some divine, but their personhood is never in doubt, simply because it is the action of reaching out to the other in love that makes them personal. Theologians and philosophers, psychologists and poets, have seen the origin of relationship in the fact of loving, the reciprocity of the self who gives and receives. In this way healing by relationship – that allows, promotes and explores the loving response of person to person – is to be considered spiritual. Jesus did not bestow healing on individuals by imparting something from outside, a privileged divine sphere which only he could enter: he enabled healing to take place *between* persons by overcoming the things that stood in its way, and by doing it from within the situation itself. The work of the Boddhisittvas was a perpetual self-giving undertaken for the joy of being of service to one's fellow men and women. The principle is the same, and it works – that is to say it has a healing effect – wherever it happens and whomever it involves.

Much of psychotherapy consists in the attempt to focus relationship, to protect it from the things that get in its way – the reification of humanness which cancels out other people's: individuality, their assimilation to a dependent position within the self, the fear that works on suggestibility for the exploitation of trust; above all, the extreme terror of exposing oneself and of being attacked when one's defences were down – all the ways that we keep ourselves from healing contact with other people, the solipsistic ploys of the infant whose urge for responsiveness has been turned in upon itself.

The intensity of being in love makes us concentrate on the privacy of the experience, particularly when we are young. But human love is never private, whatever arrangements society may make to keep it so in order to protect public order and private self-consciousness. From one point of view, of course, love is always social; it 'makes the world go round', there could be no living together in peace without it. Toleration is not enough; social life requires a degree of positive acceptance, which means that there must be, on however small a scale, actual opportunities for inter-living and mutual acceptance. Indeed, the relationship between love and social structure is fundamental to human experience; we cannot understand what society is unless we know about love and how it works. In fact, love is 'how it works'; a dynamism *among* persons which reflects a relationship of mutuality *between* persons. A critical examination of society must take into account the way that all human relationships are formed, the conditions of lasting associations between individuals. Certainly the structures of opposition and defensiveness play as large a part in the drama of action and re-action as those of mutual support and reciprocity; but these negative movements, whatever their final effect, originate in alliances of individuals and groups in which attachment is just as complete and co-operation just as loving. At every level of the structure the mechanisms of love may serve the purposes of hatred and destructiveness, for any alliance which is going to be effective in bringing about social change of any kind must first of all use love to do so; the naked individual cannot remain so, and live. At some time we must discover how to put our vulnerability to good use in gaining someone else's love. Those who are able to do this from the beginning, having been helped to do so by the example of their own mothers, are bound to be most effective in their later social relationships; but this doesn't mean that he or she will always use the skill they possess in the service of a wider love. Love is not always used *for* love.

On the other hand, responsive love and personal relationship are, from the structural point of view, the same thing. Both can be exploited, both distorted, but their origin is the same. It is the movement out towards, and back from, the other. Both society itself and individuals belonging within it, are transactional phenomena. It is the sense of personal significance, of life within a meaningful universe, that is given and received, not the simple satisfaction of so many private urges, the relief of so many examples of intra-psychic pressure. This sense of meaning is associated with awareness of the 'object', Freud's word for our mental image of another person. It is a suitable term for two reasons: if we are the subject of an experience, if it is something that is happening to us, then it is an object, even if it, the experience, is another person. But there is another sense in which the other is our 'object'. Object also means 'aim'. The aim of our organismic life is to form personal relationships. We are not isolates, wrestling with our instincts in order to reduce psychological tensions which refer only to our own interior economies; the tension we feel comes from the presence within our awareness of things we long to make contact with, people we want to know, and be known by, because it is by knowing these people and things that we come to know ourselves. Without our setting we are less than human. Growth into personhood consists of building a world. Not grabbing it, forcing it into submission, and so attempting to bond it to our will. We build our world with its own permission, in the way that we let ourselves form part of others' worlds. We are creatures who live in the worlds we build one another – such is our unspoken agreement. It has to be agreement. Worlds that are grabbed provide little shelter, and soon fall apart. It is as if they do not really belong to us, and will not work unless they do. They come furnished with meaning – meaning for us, which we accept as our meaning precisely because it is gift rather than imposition.

Dramatherapy and Relationship

In this section I shall be arguing that one of the things that give spiritual force to ordinary events and objects is drama. It does so by presenting them in holistic terms as the phenomena of personal relationships. The theoretically associated collections of data that we painstakingly arrange in systematic attempts to organise our world can never give life the meaning it craves. Only living moments of encounter can do this. Only love can do it. Dramatherapy is a spiritual therapy because, from time to time, it becomes a kind of acted mysticism, as its movements take on the form of a meditation, the procession of bodies which are movements of soul, glimpses of personal truth. Thus it is open to people 'of any religion or none'; prior belief is not necessary for this revelation. It is also open to those who are not religiously inclined – first and foremost it is a place and time of discovery, discovery about oneself and others. It provides opportunities for all kinds of personal experiences that can be shared among the group whom they concern and among whom they originate. Because of the obliqueness of its approach it brings together a wider range of people, encouraging them to find within its parameters whatever they feel is there *for them*, which includes all sorts of things they may have never expected: the limits of the hypothetical are very wide indeed, and those who embark on dramatherapy find things that they could not have been looking for as well as things they were seeking. They were not looking for them because up to now these things had no reality. Ideas and objects, works of art and natural phenomena are realised in dramatherapy by being presented as persons. The imagery of this relation is the love that is between persons here and now, the iconography of the immediate moment.

This is not to say that it exists on its own, divorced from any other kind of experience. Like everything else, love has its circumstances. The present must always be *presented*. This is done, not by describing the immediate situation, but by distancing it within the imagination. The immediate is mediated by distance; otherwise it is confused, distorted, overlooked; or it is rationalised, subsumed, included, all ways of being transformed from itself into something else. The principle seems to be the same for all our perceptions of what is apart from ourself: we can only know it as itself if we know it in terms of our ignorance rather than our knowledge. We must always say, *'The thing that I know is not this.'* Thus, we reach out to what we do not yet know, admitting that we do not yet know it. We reach *across* to it. The revelation is in the reaching, not the touching, as the touching leads so rapidly into the staking of a claim for future knowledge.

One way of 'presenting the present' is by expressing it as fiction. In other words an invented reality, which is obviously not our own, but reminds us of the world with which we are familiar, is interposed between ourselves and the familiar world, breaking our immediate engagement with it. We are aware that its setting is fictional, and has no real existential claim over us nor we over it. The setting has no purpose but that of presenting a valid insight and of disclosing its own nature as a setting. In other words it is honest about itself. Unlike the settings we provide in our ordinary experience of life, which claim to be 'true', it lacks the power to cannibalise its own experience by assimilating it to what is already known and understood and included.

This is the aesthetic distance upon which artistic experience – artistic truth – depends. It underlies Martin Buber's claim that: 'The story is itself an event and has the quality of a sacred action' (1962: 71). To take story seriously is to be aware of its nature as truthful fiction – that is both fact and fiction. The factual element consists in the straightforward description of what is happening: 'This is fiction.' The description changes the nature of the thing described, making it more of a fact, less of an invention, social fact rather than individual fantasy. Now the fiction stands forth as an invitation to flesh out the life of imagination with personal experience; we take responsibility for the dramatic structures we glibly exploit in the daily business of self-presentation.

The connection between story, the narrative presentation of events, and the place in which story is told, is vitally important. The Japanese sculptor-poet Toshikatsu Endo points to the space-creating effect of story in a way that immediately suggests dramatherapy: 'When I say that I want to create a place, I mean one that is very dense. Every people, every community, has its own place, and it is from their common stories that its density is generated' (1992). In dramatherapy, the kind of story that is to be enacted is made clear by the space generated, which in itself gives artistic significance to the story, demonstrating its identity as story, something whose meaning and importance are poetic rather than literal (see Appendix III).

The primary purpose of dramatherapy might be described as that of helping people to achieve human relationship within the right degree of nervousness and confidence. Too much nervousness, and the encounter will be blocked by being included in a limited range of things that are already well known; too much confidence and the same thing will happen, this time because in a world which remains fluid, nothing really changes. The structure of drama, however, contributes to semantic clarity by making crucial distinctions among different kinds of meaning. With clarity comes relationship – the ability to let ourselves be emotionally involved. 'We stand inextricably within the event and detached outside it, overpowered and yet observing, abandoned and preserved' (Buber, 1957: 61). We can take such a position because we know what is happening. The rules of the game are clear, clearer than they are in many of the situations we are involved in outside the dramatic frame. Confident of the meta-message – the fictional scenario, the assumed character of the actor, the place and time set apart for a special kind of reality – we plunge into the images which are the message, the beckoning life of those who reach out towards us in what Buber calls 'The polar unity of feeling' (1957: 67).

As we saw, aesthetic distance is the awareness that art *is* art, that draws us into a closer relationship with its subject matter. Through it, an identification takes place which is mediated by imagination at a profound level, that of being rather than doing, and the result is catharsis, the 'purging of pity and fear', Aristotle's celebrated 'medical metaphor' of the dramatic event. Fear and pity are not got rid of by being unloaded on to fictional characters – although many people have assumed that this is what Aristotle meant. In fact, the very opposite happens; fear for oneself and pity for somebody else are purified ('purged') by encounter. It is as if the circumstances of the drama intensify our natural ability to 'stand in someone else's shoes' by demonstrating to us that it is in fact our separateness that permits us to do so. Separation allows us to give ourselves without fear of losing ourselves, letting our pity for another person transform our fears about ourselves so that both pity and fear become an experience of sharing. S. H. Butcher, writing in the last century, describes the process as follows: 'The emotion of fear is profoundly altered when it is transferred from the real to the imaginative world. It is no longer the direct apprehension of misfortune hanging over our own life – it is the sympathetic shudder we feel for those whose character in its essentials resembles our own' (1951: 258, 259). Aesthetic distance, which brings home to me the fact that I am *not* the other, but am *with* the other, is the very heart of drama. It is the mechanism bringing about the contextual event that is the play, in which our fears for ourselves are redeemed by a special kind of contact with others – redeemed and transformed. The artistic nature of the play sets us free from our bondage to ourselves, and hands us over to relationship with the other. *We reach out*, but we do not *take over*.

This then is the purpose of the structuralisation of drama, the painstaking effort to distinguish two separate worlds which the imagination may relate without confusing. It is to teach us about relationship-in-separation, which is the truth, primal and ultimate, about human personhood – our meeting place with one another and with God. Writing from an object relations theory point of view, David Read Johnson says that:

> The therapeutic goal is to reverse... the vicious circle of primary boundary confusion, anxiety and retreat from reality. Clearly an environment is needed in which relationship with others will be as non-threatening as possible, one with distinct boundaries and structure to ensure that the insecure personality will not be engulfed. An environment must be created in which something of the inner self may be safely expressed, so that it can be identified and later integrated with other parts of the self that have been cut off from it. (1981: 30, 51)

This is explicit enough, but it leaves out the element of surprise, of a mysterious and paradoxical event taking place, which Buber celebrates. In dramatherapy, as in any kind of drama, challenge is as important as safety: 'Drama provides a rich mixture of safe structure and open opportunity for risk-taking and spontaneity, enabling the participants to move from the known into the unknown and to experience the possibility of transformation and change within the drama' (Casson, 1990, personal communication). 'To experience the possibility': John Casson describes the phenomenon very well. It is this that invigorates and inspires. We reach out towards the other in a movement that says only 'perhaps'; we move back again to ourselves to examine what we have discovered, and find it is not what we imagined it would be; fascinated, we move outwards again, this time carrying something of our own; this is precious, but we lose it on the way, and stand bewildered until someone gives it back to us, changed. 'Salvation', says Charles Williams, 'lies everywhere in interchange' (1937: 248). To this extent, dramatherapy is to do with salvation; not because it permits us to be passively transformed, but because it gives us an opportunity to meet one another in the depth of our individual humanity, and share God's creative activity as this is expressed in human encounter: 'Man can become whole not in virtue of a relation to himself but only in virtue of a relation to another self. This other self may be just as limited and conditioned as he is; in being together the unlimited and unconditioned is experienced' (Buber, 1961: 204). Drama exploits the products of our skill and imagination in order to promote a movement outward from self to other in which all such things are left behind. The

'safety' of a fictional scenario, an assumed 'character', a place and time set
specially apart for the drama to be performed, all of them artefacts specially
devised to keep real life at arm's length, exaggerate our separation from one
another in a way that demands our involvement with them and defuses the
defensiveness which prevents encounter. Value for human beings is 'in the
space between', the separation which allows relationship. To try to live in
'Thou' is to be painfully limited by the experience of someone else's being,
restricting one's thoughts and feelings to those learned from them. To try to
live in 'It' is to forswear real personal contact, and enjoy the omnipotence
of 'pure' thought unfettered by human circumstance. Aesthetic distance
provides an experience which is neither included by, nor includes, the other;
one that is neither depressive nor schizoid (see Appendix III). In drama,
withdrawal and encounter, courage and self-preservation oscillate to maintain
a kind of relational balance of thought and experience that is genuinely
human, and, according to Buber, genuinely religious. Drama holds the
possibility of newness and life within itself like an organism preserved in
amber. In it, as in man himself, the relation 'I–Thou' perpetually becomes
'I–It' because it cannot help doing so according to the very nature of human
consciousness, which inevitably withdraws and observes until again it enters
into relation. At this point an underlying value and structural principle of
dramatherapy coincides with a particular definition of religion, that of the
Hasidic tradition: 'Every particular "Thou" is a glimpse through to the eternal
"Thou"' (Buber, 1961: 75). As I have written elsewhere, 'Art becomes the
perfect medium of religious awareness once it is understood that the work
of art depends upon, that it lives in and through, separation' (Grainger, 1974:
149).

I and Thou represent the basic requirement for relationship between
persons, whether they be human or divine. In itself, relationship is a spiritual
concept in that those who open themselves to another person are thereby
open to God. Modern Christian theology rejects traditional 'patriarchal' and
'androcentric' images of God, and dwells upon the mutuality that lives in
genuine encounter, the coming together of those who make no claims on
each other, each bestowing her or his own being as a gift to the other.
Wherever such loving openness to the other exists, spiritual awareness,
consciousness of God as the Other, makes transcendence immanent. The
enterprise of loving, in which both share, intervenes between I and Thou
expressly to prevent confusion and blurring of identity. It allows the lover to
behold the beloved perpetually as Thou, the one to whom love is directed.
Absolute love, says Richard of St Victor, demands this basic plurality of
persons: 'The essential ingredient of true charity is not merely to love the

other as one is loved oneself, and to be beloved in return, but to want the other to be loved as one is loved' (Pernoud, 1973: 76). Thus, nothing is taken at the other's expense, and everything is shared by respect for the integrity of those involved. Obviously, in order to reflect love like this, the intervening factor must be as personal as the other two; its equal participation in the love and joy of the other two is 'a requirement of the same love carried to perfection'. Interpersonal love is the love that moves between, which is the soul of both. It is on this fact of human relationship that dramatherapy depends.

The Session

The location is an Occupational Therapy Work-Room at a Regional Secure Unit. The clients are eight patients: Sandy (45), Tom (30), Philip (32), Jean (38), Shaun (40), Clem (35), Sharon (28) and Stuart (30). There are three nurses: Rachel (28), Greg (25) and David (40). Simon (50) is the therapist. Jean and Stuart have never been to a dramatherapy session before, nor have any of the nurses, who are unable to attend regularly because of their working conditions. (The strict supervision required by a unit like this one renders the presence of nursing staff compulsory. This causes a problem, because it never seems to be the same nurses for two sessions in a row!) It is the seventh session in which the group has met. Sessions normally begin with a kind of introductory phase. Today, instead of standing or sitting in a ring and rehearsing names, Simon launches out as soon as everybody has come into the room by suggesting that everyone should make his or her own introductions. They should do it in as many ways as they can think of: warmly, coldly, suspiciously, scornfully, contemptuously. Some people obviously find this hard to do, or think it silly. They begin to move out of the centre of the room. Simon changes the instructions: 'Say goodbye, then! In as many ways as possible! Think about saying goodbye!' Stuart says 'I'd like to say goodbye to this bloody place!' and people laugh. Stuart says 'I'm not staying, it's all bloody stupid. He marches out of the room, taking Jean with him. Simon shouts goodbye after him, and some of the others join in… there is a period of confusion with a certain amount of laughter and relaxation. Simon is obviously thinking of ways to make therapeutic use of the situation (though stricter attention to group dynamics would probably have prevented the situation arising!) The members who are left form a group in the centre of the room. All the nurses have withdrawn now: perhaps they followed Stuart and Jean.

Sandy, who is very polite and rather shy, says 'Well, that was a surprise, wasn't it?' Clem says 'Life's full of surprises!' Tom says 'Not many surprises here'. Simon takes the hint and suggests that people invent scenes which depend on surprises: stories with a twist in the tale, beginnings with surprising endings. He stresses the point he has made: 'You start out with everyone expecting something and then something quite different happens.' This seems a good idea in the circumstances, and the members form two groups to work on the theme. One group consists of Sandy, Philip and Shaun; the other of Tom, Clem and Sharon. The second group are first to come up with an idea: two men trying to pick up a glamorous stranger, only to discover that it's a policeman in 'drag'. They show this to the first group, who are very impressed, but still can't think of anything. Simon says 'Just imagine something different. Some*thing*, some*body*, some*where*.' Sandy says 'That's the trouble I can't think of anything. It must be this place.' Tom says 'I can imagine something different from here.' Simon suggests that, instead of thinking up a sketch, people have a go at saying what they would imagine a perfect place to be like. What sort of characteristics would it have? Sharon says 'Well, it would be like heaven, wouldn't it?'

SIMON: 'What would that be like, then?'

TOM: 'Miles away from here.'

CLEM: 'This is daft.'

SIMON: 'I don't think it is. What do you think a place like that would be like, Clem? What sort of things would go on there?'

CLEM: 'Justice, and equality. And peace...'

SHARON: 'And love.'

TOM, SANDY AND PHILIP: 'Yes, love.'
           (Pause)

PHILIP: 'People understanding one another.'

SIMON: 'Accepting one another, d'you think?'

SANDY: 'Yes, accepting, that's very important.'

Simon asks everybody to draw up a chair so that they form a circle in the middle of the room. He invites people to make themselves as comfortable as they can, saying that they can keep either their eyes open or close them, according to how they feel. He explains that the chairs are their island in the middle of the sea. People are to imagine that it is their place, the place where the things they have been describing are in charge – there is justice and equality among everybody, and people really love one another. (Tom:

'And peace!') Simon pauses. After a few seconds he says 'I'm kicking my feet
through the warm dry sand.' Almost immediately Sharon says 'I'm sitting on
a rock, dangling my feet in the water. It's a pool and I can see fish in it.'
No-one says anything, so she continues: 'Those tropical fish like you see in
Chinese restaurants.' Philip: 'Perhaps this is where they come from.' There
is a long pause, much longer than the group can normally sustain. Suddenly,
when it seems as though people may have fallen asleep, Clem says 'Look at
the trees' and Philip says 'They always look like that at this time in the day.'
A conversation ensues between the two men, in which Philip says he doesn't
think he'll bother to go to work today, and Clem tells him not to be silly, he
hasn't any work to go to, and Philip replies that he has, he's building a dam
at the lagoon. Simon says that one of them has stolen something from
someone else's belongings, what are they going to do about it? After a pause
Clem says 'We haven't got any belongings.'

SIMON: 'Well they did something wrong, it doesn't matter what
            they did.'

SHARON: 'Forgive them.'

SIMON: 'Just like that?'

SANDY: 'Perhaps we ought to find out why they did it?'

TOM: 'It would make a difference what it was.'

SANDY: ·'We'd do it kindly, so they didn't feel bad about it, but
            never did it again.'

After another pause, Simon says, 'I like it here' and everyone else says 'So
do I'. Philip says 'I hope we're not rescued.' Simon explains that no-one
knows where they are. 'We can never leave.' 'Good,' says Sandy. Simon
suggests that they could build a boat and Philip says that he thinks it might
be a good idea. The group mime building a boat, chopping down trees and
using their bodies to represent the framework. When the boat has been built,
each person chooses something to take away from the island. This can be an
object, an idea or a feeling. They do this privately, without saying what they
have chosen. The boat casts off, and they sail to the shore. A storm arises,
pushing the chairs around and masking the island from view. When they
arrive 'home', they show one another the things that they have brought back
with them, and say how they are going to use them in their ordinary lives.
Tom has brought 'relaxation' back, Sandy has a leaf and a flower – 'because
I'll need the beauty' – Philip has brought 'friendship', Shaun has rescued
some silver sand in half a coconut shell: 'I don't know why, it just seems to
sum things up.' Clem has brought 'peace and love', and Sharon has done the

same. They promise to share these things with one another and as many other people as they can. The group says goodbye and undertakes to meet again next week.[1] 'The chief concern is not with... analysis and reflection, but with the true original unity, the lived relation' (Buber, 1966: 18).

---

1   The shape of this session is worth noticing, conforming as it does to the rite of passage model (Van Gennep, 1960): the *central liminal section*, 'on the island' is established by two triads of events, one preceding and one following. The pre-liminal triad consists of (a) saying goodbye in various ways, (b) the confusion of people going at different speeds and times, (c) practise in getting used to the idea of a new experience. *The post-liminal triad* consists of (a) building the boat, (b) 'destroying the island' (moving the chairs), c) bringing things back to their ordinary uses.

CHAPTER 3

Shamans and Shamanism

'Shaman' is a Siberian word, referring to a kind of religious system which originated in Central Asia among the hunter peoples and spread westward into Europe and eastward across Siberia into Alaska and thence to North and South America. The characteristic feature of shamanism is curing illness by means of a 'spiritual journey' undertaken by the shaman, who is trained in theatrical self-presentation. In his or her person the shaman links the two roles of healer and spiritual intermediary. It has been said that 'shamanism is the branch of doctoring that is religious; and the kind of religion... that is theatrical' (Schechner, 1988: 122). Thus shamanism combines three world-views: the therapeutic, the spiritual and the dramatic. Shamans are involved in ceremonies of exorcism in which the forces causing mental and bodily illness are defeated with 'power from on high'. In his thesis on 'Shamanistic elements of oriental theatre' (1978), which deals mainly with shamanism in Sri Lanka, John Casson describes how the shamanic function 'develops in various roles: medium, prophet, poet, diviner, sorcerer, dancer, actor etc.' The shaman dances in order to go into a trance, during which his 'journey' is believed to take place. The vivid setting for this is made up of symbols of the return of the spirit world, centred upon the 'tree that connects heaven and earth which grows at the world's centre', the point where time begins. Eliade describes the shaman as 'ascending to heaven and descending to hell'. Certainly the presentation is theatrical. Casson describes a *Thovil* exorcism ceremony he witnessed in 1976:

> The patient snarls, growls, screams, raises her fists against the terrific, funny black demon who shakes his arse, opens his jaw, staring with terrific eyes; wild dangerous black hair, big teeth. The patient stares at her 'hallucination' – her real vision which is to be defeated so that she may be freed and restored.

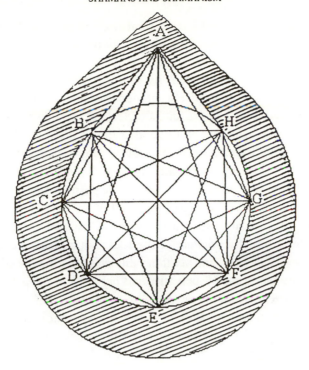

 The 'relational area'

Group Holism: the 'relational area', of the group is felt to be more than the sum of the interactions of its members (A–H). A has become the focus of group awareness, and has shaman-like significance for the group. The spiritual identity of the group corresponds to its 'relational area'.

Figure 3.1. Group Holism

The shaman usually begins his or her performance in the nude, or only partially dressed, in order to be able to get into role along with donning her or his own special costume. Curtains and blindfolds add to the atmosphere of dramatic surprises and the entrance to other worlds. 'If the white cloth is symbolic of the world of the dead, to disappear behind a white curtain may be the equivalent of a trance journey to the underworld.' Casson concludes that 'It is a short step from the Thovil to the drama' (1978: 153).

And yet this candid use of theatre embodies a most serious purpose. The exorcism ceremonies seek to deal with the dark powers that exert power over the minds of men and women, not only according to 'primitive' folk-lore and religious enthusiasm, but in the thinking of such writers as C.G. Jung, who vividly describes how the mind's balance can be upset by archetypes of the collective unconscious that demand individual expression. The following passage describing the action of psychic archetypes seems particularly relevant to the shamanic theatre: 'As the archetypes, like all numinous contents (of the mind) are relatively autonomous, they cannot be integrated simply by rational means, but require a dialectical procedure, a real coming to terms with them.' He goes on to say that this is 'often conducted by the patient in dialogue form. Usually the process runs a dramatic course... accompanied by dream symbols that are related to the "*représentations collectives*" which in the form of mythological motifs, have portrayed psychic processes of transformation since the earliest times.' (1959: 40, 41) Thus the ceremonies of Sri Lankan shamans are acted icons of psychological truth; their dramatic form externalises dramas of the soul taking place at another level than that of every day life, and yet inevitably affecting the life of every day in ways that are subtle and all-pervasive and *impossible to deal with at that level*.

Richard Schechner has drawn attention to the way that drama becomes ritual at the point at which the division between spectator and performer is lost in the rising tide of identification and the audience begins consciously to realise its solidarity with the actors. The ritual dimension of shamanism is of the greatest importance, as important in fact as the theatrical aspect. Certainly it would be misleading to regard what is happening solely in terms of psychological self-exposure. This would be to approach shamanism too directly and to overlook its real nature as dramatherapy. These are religious dramas into whose world everybody is drawn. There is a qualitative change, sometimes amounting to a cosmological shift.

Shamanism is half-way between the realised fantasy of theatre and the corporate intentionality of ritual. Theatrical structure distances us from the other as source of alienation, leaving us open to the other as relational event. In ritual, however, all are performers, and the distance separates everyone who takes part from the otherness to which they reach out. It is distance that is displaced. Whereas theatre reaches *between*, ritual reaches *beyond*. The figure of the shaman links the imaginative power of theatre to the consciousness of social belonging associated with ritual. It has been said that the figure of the shaman, or healing intermediary between human and spiritual worlds, plays a crucial role in the development of theatre (Casson, 1978). Certainly, human rituals are very old indeed, almost certainly older than any kind of theatre that we have records of; because they resemble animal rites and seem to be used for identical purposes of communicating an intention or desire to act rather than the action itself, we are justified in regarding them as the oldest kind of corporate symbolic performance. Lorenz says that:

The formation of traditional rites must have begun with the first dawning of human culture, just as at a much lower level phylogenitive rite formation was a prerequisite for the origin of social organisation in higher animals... In both cases a behaviour pattern by means of which a species in one case, a cultured society in the other... acquires an entirely new function, that of communication'. (1967: 72–3)

He goes on to draw attention to typical characteristics of ritual behaviour – 'rhythmical repetition', for example, and 'mimic exaggeration'.

The shaman is the focus of ritual behaviour. In an important sense, the special ways of moving and speaking, acting and reading associated with ritual are modelled on him or her – we act in her or his drama. The personal gives birth to the corporate, which in turn becomes personal. A shaman is one who is present among us rather than over against us, as in drama, leading rather than fascinating and involving. The experiences of shamans are fantastic, abnormal, an exaggerated version of the feelings and aspirations of the group. Although vividly real on one level, on the level of feelings that are shared they construct a world which defeats disbelief by sheer pressure of sensation rather than seducing its suspension by imaginative involvement. Here, everything is larger or smaller, faster or slower, than life and so, despite its strangeness, less psychologically threatening. This is what I mean by the 'distancing' – a disarming of fantasy by exaggerating power over the feared object, which is controlled by manipulation and distortion.

At the same time, the ritualised gestures draw attention to the intentionality of the actors, pointing out that what is going on is of intense public importance; it is larger than life and able to change life. The hunter-shaman wanders triumphantly through the forest leading behind him his train of ferocious animals and terrifying monsters. Australian aborigines construct rites and ceremonies from what a shaman 'sees' either while asleep or alone in the desert. The shaman's experience becomes the material for their transformation. He takes the dangers of experience, spiritual and physical, real and fantastical, upon himself in order to exorcise them on their behalf and, in a sense, in their persons. In Schechner's phrase, 'A shaman is a professional link connecting disparate but interacting reality spheres.' He goes on to say that 'One of the ways a person knows that s/he is going to become a shaman is when s/he experiences visions that can be translated into performances' (1988: 219). These performances are the ritualisation of a drama constructed by the shaman out of his or her own imaginative being and realised in the action of sharing within the group. Thus the shaman is link person in the ritual which represents the group's aspirations and intensions. She or he does not simply perform on behalf of the group;

theatricality draws the audience across the footlights to participate in the reality of the drama as virtual members of the cast. Here the whole group shares the joys and pains, the terror and exultation of the journey (see Figure 3.1).

Religious ecstasy, says Eliade, is probably 'co-existent with the human condition' (1965: 101). The distinguishing mark of shamanism is the use to which it is put. The shaman is a bringer of healing to others. His or her ecstasy bridges the gap between the sufferer and the source of wholeness. Because this idea finds expression within the language of ritual, it takes the form of an actual journey forwards and backwards between two points, the famous 'magic flight' of shamanism, passed on from generation to genera-tion: 'The instruction of the fledgling shaman first by elder shamans and then by the spirits is a universal aspect of shamanism.' It is a long training involving initiation into an exacting spiritual universe. 'These journeys', says Schechner, 'are neither gratuitous nor for private use. He goes to get something and he must deliver what he gets back to his people – he must teach them what he learns. His work is social work' (1988: 42). It is purposeful and goal-orientated but by no means automatic, a matter of communication rather than manipulation, the harmonising of intention and awareness to permit a healing encounter to take place. Transformation is by means of living experience not by the magical exercise of power. Because it stresses its own theatricality, requiring imaginative involvement rather than technical skill in the construction of a new social universe, it brings ritual into the realms of drama. Both Kirby (1975) and Casson (1978) see theatre as originating in shamanism; Eliade describes how the shaman 'turns himself into an animal just as he achieves a similar result by pulling on an animal mask' (1970: 93). In other words he or she identifies imaginatively with the role he or she plays, redefining his or her own personal reality in terms of the mask that is worn, just as actors do in so many of the theatrical traditions of the world. The effect of the mask is a powerful reflexivity, an experience of being taken over rather than assuming control.

What the shaman 'sees' when in character is expanded into ritual performed by the tribe. Read describes how the shamanic event originates in an experience of sharing among the members of the group: 'Thus sustained, I was one of innumerable companies of men who, back to the shrouded entrance of the human race, have sat at night by fires and filled forest clearings and the wilderness with recitations of their own uniqueness' (1965: 252). Among such spiritual explorers are those who acquire real knowledge which they proceed to bring back and share with the community. The increase in scale that the narrative assumes is, like all ritual, defensive as well as aggressive. What appears to be an attempt to give an impression of superiority is, in fact, an admission of weakness; those involved 'play at' being bigger, stronger, wiser, fiercer. The artificiality of their attempts proclaims vulnerability rather than real confidence in any ability to carry off the kind of things they mimic. At the same time, however, there is an intention of encounter, a desire to be engaged, to present themselves face to face with the situation that they are involved with and that they perceive to be to some extent a matter of life and death. Like the rituals of some other social animals, these patterns express a dangerous state of affairs rendered harmless by deflection into behaviour that is non-functional and yet full of meaning – the *reduction ad absurdum* of a corporate intention.

This game-playing is a special kind of reality, a shift of frame from the instrumental world into the dramatic world of 'as if', in which ideas and feelings about a non-existent state of affairs become the common property of a whole group of people to be lived as temporary *ad hoc* social reality. By common consent, the frame of individual experience has been shifted and the social awareness that authenticates our actions and reactions, making them 'real' to us gives a special significance to the games we play, the dramas we construct. At a very deep level these games and dramas – the difference is only one of the degree to which we structure reality – serve a primary purpose of human solidarity. They are excuses for making contact with one another in order to enjoy the healing that such basic contact brings. What is 'only a game', 'only a play' can disarm our self-protectiveness and turn us towards one another in a way that nothing else can. It is not the game or the play that does this, but the awareness that it is a game or a play, giving us the confidence to reach out to one another without having to go farther than we really want to go, and exposing more of our real selves than we normally choose to do in such circumstances.

And then it is blessedly too late. The play that lays seize to our emotions, the game that fascinates our intellect, becomes the shared experience, the rite. We feel its urgency and are committed. Our defences are destroyed. Jacob Moreno, the originator of psychodrama, coined the word 'tele' to describe the sharing that takes place in a group bound together by dramatic reality (1946). The structure of the group allows communication at a level which is deeper than conscious thought or feeling. There is an interchange of unconscious experience involving the release of underlying psychological urges. Moreno's experience with psychodrama gives substance to the psychological theories of Ian Suttie (1988), who pointed out that for human beings togetherness is at the heart of things, not an optional extra, or the by-product of the instinctual pleasure principle. This is purposeful action, the expression of the urge to be involved in the creation of meaning out of confusion, community out of isolation. It is not a by-product of anything at all, but produces its own effects, transmits its own messages, messages both concerning and on behalf of itself. Certainly it is the expression of a socio-formative intention, fragmented to begin with, but gaining coherence, but this is its principle purpose, and any secondary effects such as the kathartic release of tension only contribute to this.

The prototype of the therapeutic group is to be found in the corporate games we played as children which offered challenge and security and, above all, the inestimable human satisfaction of being appreciated by our fellow players as contributing members of the group, secure and loved. In those games, we had every reason to take part and none to hang back. Certainly we had to find our level of skill but there were rules to tell us what to do and how and when to do it. One thing that the dramatherapy group does is to remind those taking part of the blessedness of rules whose fundamental structured purpose is clearly revealed in a way that seldom happens in other settings. The game *is* the rules – a certain interaction of principles and procedures which takes all freedom of action within the game into itself. Those in the game actively embrace its structure; there is nothing else they can do. Losing themselves in the skilled manipulation of structure, they find a freedom from the anxiety of self-presentation whilst at the same time they are obliged to acknowledge and be acknowledged by the other people in the group. These other people are not merely spectating or interested parties, but the objects and subjects of the rules, the social organisation for whom the rules exist.

Such is the case with games that have been made up beforehand, the kind that might be used as a way of 'warming up' a dramatherapy group; people's fears of being caught off guard and not knowing what to do, their painful inability to 'join in', are overcome by the satisfaction of having something to do that doesn't really matter ('after all, it's only a game') and that no-one does very well. If it makes people laugh, so much the better. Later on, of course, a group will devise its own games, in which the element of competition will almost certainly be more pronounced, but the overall satisfaction is greater as people discover the pleasure of working together to create something to which all have contributed, in which everybody's individuality is expressed: 'A special world is created where people can make the rules, rearrange time, assign values, and work for pleasure. This "special world" is not gratuitous, but a vital part of human life.' Richard Schechner concludes that 'no society, no individual, can do without it' (1988).

This special atmosphere of the game, combining security and freedom and mutual celebration, provides the setting for adventure of a kind which is necessary for the achievement of personhood. Games stretch reality by introducing their own rules, which override 'ordinary' social behaviour. The game is safe and dangerous at the same time. It is safe because, although success or failure will be a matter of personal – and social – significance, its meanings are clear and their significance subscribed. It has a graspable urgency and can be mastered or abandoned. It is dangerous because of the rigour of its demands. You cannot half-play a game. Playing badly is something else; to play badly is to fail altogether. The circumscribed importance of the game produces the kind of concentration that leads to the transcendence of ordinary expectations. We are swept along by the impetus of the event and find ourselves running faster than we expected – faster than we thought we could run. On this well-trodden ground we rise to unplanned heights of self-awareness, mutual celebration and, consequently, implications for personal growth.

Both elements, the dramatic and the ritual, contribute to the unique exposure of those involved in playing group games, the first representing personal relationship, the second, group solidarity. To put this another way, the drama portrays life while the rite mirrors perfection; in its flexibility and rigidity, its solemn concentration and its hilarity, the game contains both. Much depends on the agreed structure – the game's 'meaning' – as in the rituals of the shamans in which a shared system of symbols is portrayed by a cast of 'mythological beings'. Just as much, however, originates in the individual contributions of those taking part, producing a cat's cradle of ideas and feelings, memories and hopes – a semi-serious recapitulation of a hundred different relationships. Again, the action of reliving is only semi-serious, concerning that part of the awareness that imagines and participates, entertaining an experience without losing hold of the frame of social reality that contains and presents it. This is the mood of much drama and dramatherapy in which the imagination expands to occupy all the space provided for it, which is the dramatic area of 'as if', and never really leaves that area. The game, like the play, exists to give depth and meaning to this epistemological shift whereby we move into another human reality, that of actions, thoughts and feelings in which it is not the experience but the circumstances which are imagined.

When we have reached this point we have moved out of the area of games where rules which are unbending determine a way of life which is not, into that of drama and ritual, when the significance of the action overflows the circumstances in which it happens. The element of 'let's pretend' is located in a different place in the rite than it is in the drama. Instead of 'let's pretend this is the real world, the one outside the theatre', it is 'let's pretend we can engage in conversation with God'. Both involve the enterprise of committing oneself to a kind of awareness that is specially adapted to the purpose in hand; an interiorised sensibility which avoids distraction and commits itself to 'living' a particular kind of relationship, the expression of transforming ideas.

Casson's description of *Gammadu* and *Thovil*, the Sri Lankan shamanistic exorcism rituals, throws light on the dramatic power ritual commands when it takes the form of theatre and draws on the imagination of everyone present. I. M. Lewis (1971) has defined the shaman as 'an inspired prophet and healer, a charismatic religious figure with the power to control the spirits'. In these rituals, magico-religious belief in the ability of the shaman to enlist the aid of spiritual forces against the malignancy of the *yakas* (evil spirits) is magnified by the kind of identification with the personages of the drama that belongs to theatre, so that the emotional impact of the performance reaches a level not usually attained in religious ritual – except perhaps in the central movement in the rite of passage, where initiates are totally enclosed in a chaotic world of drastic change without any of the familiar signs to orientate themselves by. These theatrical rituals of Sri Lanka are located within the everyday world rather than outside the camp in a setting specifically chosen with the intention of keeping the rest of life at arms' length. Their effect comes from aesthetic distance rather than the systematic manipulation of the total environment which present the familiar world as a phantom memory rather than a real possibility. In shamanistic dramas the world is changed by sympathy, according to the principles of Aristotle who points out that it is because we do not have to get involved that we do in fact do so, binding our own reality to the action presented before us, permitting its world to influence the reality of our own. Casson speaks of 'the hypnotic, ecstatic power of inspiration' of the Sri Lankan dance-drama. Earlier in his account he describes how one of the shamanic performances 'frightened me more than I have ever been in a theatre'. The excited action within the scene is mirrored in the turbulent mood of the audience. 'For all present, shamanism is a set of experiences of a very powerful kind... I was thrilled to see something that seemed to point to the very origins of drama: a Dionysian, hilarious, obscene play, mixing ecstasy, trance, wildness and laughter, intoxication and performance' (*Sokari*, folk play) (1978: 68, 12, 7). Shamanic ritual combines drama, dance, acrobatics, mime and many other pictorial, aural and tactile media within a scenario where scope is earth, heaven, hell and paradise. It is terrifying and hilarious. Casson describes the masked drama known as *Kolam* as 'communal therapy' (1978: 195) and this dimension of social healing characterises the shamanic tradition in which a whole community is inspired and renewed in the person of the individual receiving exorcism. In the folk play *Sokari*, for instance, not only Sokari himself but also members of the audience went into a healing trance (1978: 306). It is by inducing trance states that shamanic theatre has its healing effect. 'It is in the trance that archetypes possess men and women. The personal consciousness is eclipsed and greater, universal, powerful figures appear – gods, demons, spirits' (Casson, 1978: 11). Casson points out that in these trance states emotional pressure and spiritual experience speak the same language. The figure of the shaman focuses and identifies the 'flow of spirit' as, encouraged by the involvement of the group, he or she voyages to the Place of Spirit and returns to share his gifts with the group for healing to take place: In McNiff's phrase, 'The group increases the power of the shamanic process with its energy' (1988: 289) and individual therapy becomes corporate renewal. 'In that night something is forged. A new order is created, the shattered form of mind is rebuilt, the disintegrated personality reassembled, the fragmented skeleton is remade and something new is implanted.' Part of its therapeutic effect derives from the systematic attempt to make people laugh, which 'reflects the psychotic, inside out, upside down craziness of the deranged person's experience. The clown heals madness by being mad' (Casson, 1978: 12, 264) so that he can lead the patient back to sanity.

The action of dramatherapy resembles this. In dramatherapy, too, the group lends its imaginative life to the shaman. From the atmosphere of sharing that its playing creates, the group may choose a spokesperson to embody its identity, to suffer and be healed on their behalf and share her/his experiences with them. This is not necessarily the role of the group leader although he or she may be the first to assume it. The whole is a kind of corporate therapy which the imagination shares and to which theatre gives life.[1]

The Session

This is an evening group which meets at the Day Hospital where rooms are let out for various purposes in the evenings. None of the members is a patient

---

1 'The creative arts therapies are contemporary manifestations of ancient continuities in art, health and religion' (McNiff, 1988: 285). Writing in the same issue, Moreno draws attention to 'a renewed awareness and appreciation of our (i.e. arts therapists') shamanic heritage.' 'There has been', he continues, 'an ever-expanding awareness of the roots of the creative arts therapies in traditional healing practices' (1988, 299–300).

at the hospital, and they have all had some previous experience of
dramatherapy. Adrian, Beryl, David and Elaine are married (though not to
each other) and aged between 30 and 40. Freda is an unmarried 65 year old
and George is 60, also unmarried. Hugh and Isabel are newlyweds in their
late twenties. Jimmy is the dramatherapist. Adrian and David and their wives,
and Elaine and her husband all attend the same Anglican church; Hugh and
Isabel are Roman Catholics. The group is particularly interested in spirituality. This is their sixth weekly meeting: the future has been left open on
purpose as it is felt that to restrict the course to a definite number of weeks
might limit people's imagination unnecessarily. A rule of this group is that
members should not speak to each other before the session is declared to
have started. This seemed awkward to begin with and the rule was almost
changed back to the previous friendly informality. The older members of the
group still feel it to be strange and unnecessary, but go along with it quite
cheerfully – it was, after all, a group decision, aimed at 'setting the scene'.
As soon as they arrive people start to re-familiarise themselves with the room
and the things that have been done and said there.

> JIMMY: 'It's seven o'clock and we're all here except Tony who said
> he couldn't come tonight. Hello. Let's say hello, let's tell
> each other how it has been. See if you can be relaxed and
> self-confident, never mind listening, just speak. Shout if
> you don't think you're being heard. Make sure they under-
> stand you. Come on then, how's it been? Since last week?'

There are a few minutes of noisy greeting and exchange of information.
People slowly drift into the centre of the room and stand grinning foolishly
at each other.

> JIMMY: 'What's been happening then? Anything interesting?'

> ISABEL AND HUGH: 'George went to Tesco.'

> GEORGE: 'I did more than that. I told you, I had to have my feet
> done. I bet you just sat at home and gazed into each
> other's eyes!' (*People laugh at this and make various comments
> such as:* 'Well, why not?' (FREDA); 'Lucky for some'
> (ADRIAN); 'Don't tease them' (ELAINE).)

> ISABEL: 'As a matter of fact we spent most of the week digging in
> the garden. So we're tired and happy.'

> DAVID: 'I went into the Peak District on Saturday, the White Peak.
> Took a bus to Buxton and walked.'

> JIMMY: 'Do you often do that, David?'

DAVID: 'Go into the country and walk? Yes. I can't walk as far as I
             could, of course. I used to walk for miles, all round
             Dovedale and Tideswell and Longnor.'

JIMMY: 'Lovely names.'

DAVID: 'I used to walk with Joanne.'

There is a slight pause, hardly perceptible. Everybody knows that Joanne
was David's wife, who died five years ago.

ELAINE: 'I suppose it must... No, go on, Freda...'

FREDA: 'It's amazing how places remind you of people...'

Several people take this idea up, to the extent of agreeing verbally or nodding
their heads. Jimmy suggests that the group might like to explore the idea a
little. The split into two teams, each acting as the audience to the other, and
begin to work on the idea of using themselves and one another, and the
various objects and pieces of furniture as materials out of which to construct
a countryside that they have particularly enjoyed, choosing someone to
represent the person they associate with it. Because time is limited, these
scenarios are only rather brief sketches. Not everybody chooses a memory,
but no-one declines to help in someone else's sketch. People start comparing
places they have known which were lost.

ISABEL: 'We could play a game about it. Someone thinks of a place
             they like and stands in the centre. The next person thinks
             of a place they like better and stands above the first person.

             They have to say why their place is better. We go on until
             everyone's involved and there's a line of places strung out
             across the room. If you disagree with the order of the
             grouping you're free to rearrange it, so long as you give a
             reason. If you can't think of anything, you're "out".'

This works quite well and there is a good deal of laughter, particularly when
the game is played with reference to places people *don't* like. David becomes
deeply involved in the action.

DAVID: 'Some places you never forget, do you?'

JIMMY: 'What like, David? What kind of places?'

David describes how, in the months after his wife's death, he had gained a
lot of comfort from the writings of the Prior of the Taizé Abbey in northern
France and had developed a deep spiritual need to visit the place where he
lived.

DAVID: 'Joanne had been many years ago. It was she who put me on
           to him. The more I thought about it, the more I longed to
           go.'

FREDA: 'Tell us about it, David.'

DAVID: 'Can I? I won't find it easy, you know.'

JIMMY: 'I think we'd like you to have a go, wouldn't we?'

People nod their heads or murmur agreement.

DAVID: 'Well, I will if you'll sit down and promise not to interrupt.'

David sits down in the middle and begins to describe the French abbey,
telling how and when it was founded and going into detail about the 'daily
routine'.

DAVID: 'The music is amazing. It has to be heard to be believed. It's
           out of this world, as they say.'

However, it was Br Roger, the founder, whom David wanted to see. His story
grew in excitement and tension as he described how he searched for the
Prior until, when he thought he would have to go home without really seeing
him properly, he discovered him in a secluded garden, early in the morning.
He hadn't spoken to him – he didn't need to.

DAVID: 'I want you to be Br Roger [*to George*] and I want you [*to
           Isabel*] to be me. I want the rest of you to be the garden just
           under the brow of the hill. You stand about here, George,
           looking away over the trees, towards the rising sun. Will
           you be the sun, Freda? What happens is that I come round
           the corner, into the garden and I just see him standing
           there.'

He has begun to weep. Now he finds that he can't go on talking. George,
Isabel and Freda act the scene out. Nobody speaks. After gazing at the sun
for a few seconds George turns round and sees Isabel standing staring at him.
He raises his hand in instinctive salute.

DAVID: 'How do you know he did that? How could you know?'

Without David's unspoken permission the other members of the group begin
to change places with the original three, until everyone has been Roger,
David or the rising sun. David sits and watches, re-living the experience. 'We
have all been', says Hugh. 'We were all there.'

The group take hands and sit in silence. Some are weeping; some smiling.
After some minutes have passed, they all stand and embrace. As is the custom
of this group, they leave in silence.

In this example, a group member took on the shamanic role, ministering to the group through his own spiritual experience. What took place may seem very different from the ceremonies described by Casson. The humour is there and the spirit of playing games. There was also a good deal of spontaneity, what Moreno calls 'The locus of self, allowing self to expand' (McNiff, 1988: 286). The extremes of experience, however, appear to be missing. For example, Claire Schmais describes the initiatory scenario of an Avam Samyoyed shaman as follows: 'At one stage he is in hell where he meets a naked man tending a fire. The man caught him with a hook, cut his head and chopped his body to bits and put him all in a kettle. There he boiled the body for three years and finally forged him a head on an anvil' (McNiff, 1988: 282). Surely this never happened to David.

In a sense it did, however, or something analogous to it (as indeed is the case with regard to the Samoyed shaman). This sort of imagery does not form part of our cultural heritage. Not until now, that is. Cinema and television are widening and deepening our symbolic vocabulary. Also, although music was mentioned it was not actually played and this constituted a considerable handicap: 'Without music, shamans in most cultures would find it difficult to travel to the spirit world' (Moreno, 1988: 276). The fact that all present were weeping, however, is culturally significant. There was no talk on this occasion about David's loss of his beloved wife and the agonies of liminality into which this event had plunged him. When he led the group in this session, however, he had passed through a major life change, and was able to share the results of a successful passage with the rest of the group.

In fact, the comparison with dramatherapy rests mainly on the central elements of shared healing within the whole group. Individual healing rituals like Thovil are actually community dramas. Casson says:

> We must not consider these particular ceremonies [the shamanic exorcisms] as apart from community ceremonies, as in western society we segregate our private therapeutic work from such community events as galas and fêtes. All ceremonies, individual and community, are concerned with the exorcism of evil/illness and the encouragement of fertility/confidence/energy. They combine to a lesser or greater degree the sublime and the ridiculous... The public nature of the event reinforces and supports the patient, enhancing their status and reintegrating the individual with his or her social group. (1984: 11)

Thus, although these dramas are open to the public in a way that dramatherapy is not, the aim of therapy through theatre is the same, and aesthetic distance, the vital separation of audience and actor, is at the heart of both. In dramatherapy it is the rest of the group that represents the community with whom the performers are reconciled; Sri Lankan players communicate with an audience which they know and are known by almost as intimately as the group members have come to know one another. The movements in which the Taizé encounter was relived took place in a kind of trance state in which spiritual awareness was intensified by sharing. The dramatherapy we know and practise draws much of its original force from a more public theatre than this, but with the same purpose, the same effect and – most important of all – identical inspiration. 'The acting out of rite, the communal activity of the performance, strengthens, invigorates, brings society together, allows for the acting out of conflicts in ritual conditions and exorcises through expression the violent, regressive, "evil" forces, the demons of society.' Casson urges us to acknowledge the source of the power which works with us for healing of persons (1984: 18). Because dramatherapy is able to manifest this underlying shamanic symbolism it comes into healing contact with the unconscious, imagined realm in which psychic individuation takes place. This most vital area of human life cannot be analytically reduced, scientifically observed or empirically tested for effects. In other words, it cannot be grasped at all; but, as we shall see in the following chapters, it may sometimes be visited.

CHAPTER 4

The Sojourn in Heaven

This dramatherapeutic approach is concerned with the rediscovery of meaning through the search for new spiritual experiences. Healing is regarded as:

> That process through which persons assign significance and meaning to each experience of their lives and their lives as wholes. This entails a constantly shifting state of awareness which encompasses the physical, emotional, mental, imaginational, environmental and spiritual events occurring in any given movement, and is establishing constantly the connection of these events with patterns of meaning which have previously appeared to the person. (Sussman, 1984)

Linda Sussman's vision of healing 'within the global moment' relates to ideas about psychological restoration and wholeness associated with Viktor Frankl (1973, 1975). If an emotionally sick person can bring him or herself to begin searching for healing, then that person will be healed. The healing is in the search itself; the search is a state of being that bestows health.

If this is so, and Dr Frankl provides a mass of evidence that is is, the problem becomes the practical one of getting distressed people to embark on a search which they feel to be pointless: 'Patients ask "What's the purpose?", "What's it for?". This arises from the very beginning of therapy, before therapy has really begun at all. They want to know what the purpose is of moving into a new kind of activity' (Alida Gersie, in conversation with the author). In dramatherapy the existential movement is embodied in a real series of actions symbolising entry into a different sphere of being. Dramatherapy is particularly appropriate as a way of searching for meaning because it is an actual, acted movement, something felt and seen to be done. The theory behind it is that if you are able to enter a new experiential space, this itself is a proof that existential alternatives exist. The dramatic framework is the means of approach. (A non-theatrical example might be the part played by fairs and carnivals within our own culture.)

Alida Gersie points out that the movement into and away from the special place of meaning are similar movements. They obey the same rules. The three stages are:

1. The entrance to Being.

2. Being.

3. The entrance to Leaving.

Change takes place on each of the two thresholds, where the connection occurs between the self as it is, and the alternative condition. Just as to pass from 1 to 2 is to move from 'death' (my present state) to 'life' (the presence of healing, of participation in the 'search for meaning'), so the transition from 2 to 3 is a real one, just as difficult to achieve. This time the passage is from 'life' to 'death'; but it is as hard to move out from the centre as to move into it. This is because we are not moving into and out of an idea but a reality: 'Because drama is a virtual reality which stands in relationship with actual reality, the questions it evokes – why should I join in, why I should stay here, what is true, what is false? – will always be the same' (Gersie, in conversation).

Thus the heart of the dramatherapy session will be an image of the Platonic Ideal: not the truth itself but the place of truth, the experience of searching which is human meaning. If it were the object of the search no-one would ever leave, seduced back into the ordinary world at the end of the session by a cup of coffee. All the same, the experience of having opened ourselves to the implications of our longing for wholeness and spiritual fulfilment is not easily abandoned. Certainly we know that what we have gone through is real – a real place and time, qualitatively different from any other. As Gersie says:

> When we stand back and look at the drama, it is like looking at our life in complete form, which is otherwise unattainable. Once we can get clients to come into contact with the tension between the two kinds of reality, we can break the grip exerted by the present situation upon their awareness, and give them practice in believing that what is virtually possible is actually attainable. Because drama consists in entering/being/exiting, when I take part I am consenting to the existence of being, human being-as-search, and exerting real hope about another kind of reality. By *acting my despair* I am generating hope.

During our conversation, Alida Gersie quoted Einstein's words: 'A knowledge of the existence of something we cannot penetrate, the manifestation of the profoundest reason and the most radiant beauty, which are only accessible to our reason in their most elementary forms – it is this knowledge and this emotion that constitute the truly religious attitude' (1935: 4, 5).

Therefore, in order to bring home the reality of the crucial difference between the three stages, Gersie divides each of the two liminal phases, i.e. those between 1 and 2, and between 2 and 3, into three movements. The stage of being is not simply moved into or out of; in each case there is a phase of liminal chaos or formlessness to divide what has been before from what is to come. The effect of this is to prevent any kind of merging or confusion, as the tripartite movements allow the old to empty completely before the new begins. The shape is now as follows:

1. The entrance to Being

	a – (That which is dying)	The process of idealisation A,
A	b – (Formless state)	and that of realisation B,
	c – (That which is emerging)	isolate 2 so that its
		identity does not merge with
2. Being		the reality of 1 and 3.
	a – (That which is dying)	
B	b – (Formless state)	
	c – (That which is emerging)	

3. The entrance to Leaving

Figure 4.1. The shape of existential change

Image and ideal belong together *because the first is the expression of the second.* However much stress we lay on the transcendence of the ideal universe symbolised in the drama, stating quite clearly that it is above and outside the ordinary world, it still has an ideational connection with that world and can be placed alongside it in thought and feeling. Otherwise the way we would contemplate it would be *sui generis,* inapplicable to the rest of life. The similarity is as important to us as the difference because we can only conceive of it in terms which include both, as items occurring alongside each other in our experience. We can, of course, define it as incomparable and uncategorisable, and this is what sophisticated religions actually do. But it will only be useful to us in so far as its 'beyond'ness and 'other'ness are translated into a language which makes sense to us, and can be used by us in order to talk to it and about it. Thus, we define the ideal and it redefines itself for us in image, symbol and story.

This approach is expressed mythologically in the religious patterns identified by Mircea Eliade in which heaven and earth are joined symbolically together, and time and place are transformed by contact with divinity. When such a thing happens, says Eliade, mankind is 're-integrated in his original plenitude' (1968). He describes the reproduction of extra-temporal experience through the artistic provision of a setting which is able to serve as the 'great' time, the time before time of religious myth. In such a special setting it is possible to present 'life-giving mythical events that are real and exemplary' (1968: 16–19). The setting itself is characterised by certain explicit lines of demarcation which set it apart from the ordinary world. It is hedged about with liminal presences, areas of human experience in which the difference between the ideal and the real are exaggerated. There is an obvious intention to protect the sacred identity of the theophany by distancing it in such a way; it is equally obvious that anything protected like this must be really worth investigating! Holiness attracts by repelling. Within religious experience, to set apart is to invite participation. Forbidden areas signify holiness.

The actual location of the theophany may be marked by the symbolism of place as the setting for the 'promotional event' which expresses perfection and is 'outside' time and place. There may be a reference to the cosmic tree, *Axis Mundi*, joining earth and heaven, often reproduced in the form of a mountain, or to the earth as Mother, *Tellus Mater*, imaged outwards in the ritual dancing-ground. Other symbols include the cosmogenic egg, giving birth to human reality and represented in the use of caves for worship; ladders or staircases connecting heaven and earth and rendering the sacred space holy by contact; the centre of the earth, represented by a navel-stone, *omphalos*, which expresses the idea that the divine is 'at the centre of creation'; the unity of all created things, represented by the natural unity of the earth with its products celebrated in a natural setting; the relationship between sacred places and people throughout the world, symbolised by worship at a particular shrine – all these are examples of the ability of a place to convey different kinds of message concerning the relationship between the human and the divine and to present a picture about the nature of reality in ways that are as graphic as may be. Its most vivid expression, however, remains the way it is *distinguished* from the rest of human experience; the sheer fact of its holiness which sets up a resistance against contact with everything outside its sacred scope, and at the same time focuses its magnetism.

The same principle applies with regard to dramatherapy. By setting a space and time aside as a 'safe area' in which the rules of life are significantly different from whatever holds sway outside, and making sure that the rules establishing its particularity are respected, attention is drawn to the unique nature of what is being protected. Thus, limitations to spontaneity and self-expression which at first seem an unnecessary and pretentious imposition of formality upon what is obviously going to be 'a fun event', stand out as an integral part of the total session. The limitations consist of everything which is presented as an unavoidable part of the structure of the event itself, something you have to do if you are going to take part, whether it is the need to obey rules of a game, the discipline of keeping 'in character', or simply having to stand or sit in a circle and take part as a member of the group – sometimes the hardest of all obstacles to cross. These things, and the techniques of role reversal and the substitution of bodily movement and gesture for verbal expression, signal the distinctiveness of the particular kind of event we call dramatherapy. They are rigorous and liberating at the same time. As I have said elsewhere:

> Because of its combinations of *structure* (character, plot and presentation) and *freedom* (from the demands of extra-dramatic reality), drama is experienced as liberating by those who find themselves oppressed by a narrow and restricted sense of themselves as an independent person, as in depressed states, or by their lack of any stable, recognizable image of the self (as in schizoid conditions) (Grainger, 1990).

Here, as in all religious matters, the power depends upon the symbolism. According to Jung, symbols have a mediating effect on our awareness, making sure that we are not exposed to the spiritual forces we need but cannot bear too much of (1940: 59). The protected space created by dramatherapy links earth and heaven in a symbolism which we are aware of as the mysterious setting of our reaching out to one another and to the divine. We believe that what we do is significant, because we are at the 'centre of the world' (Eliade, 1958: 51, 52), the location of birth and rebirth, the starting point and destination of the hero's journey. In such places, whatever their actual geographical setting may be, life takes on an infinitely wider significance than it usually possesses. Awareness becomes mandala-like, assuming perfect form and balance. When dramatherapy reaches this point it abandons plot for statement and dramatic action for the harmony of masque.

The Session

The setting is the main hall of a psychiatric day hospital, and the clients are Jenny (30), Mavis (50), Dawn (29), Ray (28), Ken (36), Andrew (24) and

Alan (48). These people have been coming to the hospital for several months, and have taken part in the dramatherapy sessions since the first week. Jenny, Mavis and Alan are diagnosed as suffering from depression; Dawn, Ken and Andrew have anxiety states, and Alan is considered to be schizophrenic. At the moment they are waiting for the session to begin, sitting in the chairs that are placed along the wall. Colin, the leader, would prefer them to be standing in the hall itself. They know this, but they prefer to wait until the last minute before launching into the empty space, and committing themselves to the session. They always find it hard to begin, although they say that they enjoy taking part. This time Colin meets them where they are, bringing a chair round to face them.

COLIN: 'What's been happening?'

Andrew laughs sarcastically.

COLIN: 'Not much, then. Jenny? Anything been happening for you?'

Jenny shakes her head, but says nothing.

COLIN: 'Mavis? Alan? Dawn? Ken? Ray? [*pausing between each name*].

             'Well, I can't say that much has been happening to me either.'

Andrew laughs again.

             (pause)

COLIN: 'Shall we just sit here and talk, or shall we do something?'

ANDREW: 'Oh, let's do something.'

He stands up, followed one by one, by the others.

Colin mentions the fact that it's a lovely day, and Dawn immediately says that it would be lovely at the seaside. All the clients agree, Ray saying that 'anything would be better than here'. Colin suggests that they go on talking, while they walk along the sand (i.e. round the hall). What's wrong with the hospital? It's boring, and it makes them feel like patients, 'as if we were less than people'. Alan says that 'You might just as well be dead, or really old. You have a feeling it's all over.' After a few moments Colin suggests that people should stop speaking and concentrate on walking through the sand. 'Just imagine you can feel it under your feet. If you want you can take your shoes off to feel it better.' Everybody except Alan does this. Colin describes the seashore on which they were walking: 'Now it's hard sand with the ridges of ripples: now it's soft feathery sand; now it's small pebbles, now large ones that hurt your feet, but here's a pool, a shallow one on the sand...' Everybody enjoys this and Alan lets Jenny take his shoes off. Dawn suddenly sits down: 'I've fallen in a puddle.' From this point things get livelier, with people kicking water at each other and chasing one another along the sand.

After a few moments, Colin calms them down by directing their attention outwards: 'Look at the sea.' The group hug one another, swaying and dipping in a tight bunch. Someone says 'Let's go on a voyage.' The group decide on what they will take with them, each person putting three imaginary things, either objects or qualities, in his or her bag, and explaining his or her reasons to everybody else. (Ray settles for 'patience'; Andrew takes his portable telephone, Mavis a washing machine.) They also apportion jobs for the voyage. This is done according to personal choice, rather than concern for the efficient running of the ship. There are two captains – Ken and Ray; a first mate – Mavis; a quartermaster doubling as cook – Alan; a ship's nurse – Jenny; an engineer – Andrew; and 'the bloke who turns the big wheel to steer' – Dawn. The ship sets sail. During the voyage, the group go through some of the motions that they associate with these roles. They do this rather listlessly, not having anything very definite to do. Things liven up when Colin announces the appearance of a storm. Now everybody rushes round the ship in excitement, which turns to panic when Colin announces that the storm is a typhoon, and that it is going to sink them. Jenny and Mavis want to know if there is any hope. No hope at all, says Colin: either jump over the side or go down with the ship. Everybody except Dawn decides to jump over the side; Dawn runs round the deck shrieking with terror, until Ray catches her round the waist and swings her over the side, diving in after her. Mavis and Alan hold hands and jump.

The sea is in turmoil, throwing them about so that they collide and are separated:

COLIN: 'What's it like?'

ANDREW: 'Terrible. Awful. I can't see...'

RAY: 'The water's getting in down my throat.' (*Makes noises to illustrate this.*)

COLIN: 'Don't say any more. Just let it happen.'

DAWN: 'We'll drown. We'll just drown.'

COLIN: 'See what that's like, then. See what it's like when you're drowned. See what you *find*. I'm not saying any more.'

Several minutes pass, although after all the activity it seems like a much longer period of time. Mavis and Alan lie side by side without moving, while the others explore various parts of the room in an aimless sort of way. Dawn does a kind of slow dance by herself in the centre of the hall. Realising no-one is taking any notice of her, she begins to take up more and more space, swooping and weaving from one side of the hall to the other. Ray seems to be sitting in one place, swaying backwards and forwards. (In fact he is making minimal progress across the room. How much progress can he make without seeming to move?) Some people greet each other, some glide or shuffle or lurch past without acknowledgement. Some keep well away. Alan stands where he dropped, talking to someone (God?) on his portable telephone. When it has all gone on for several minutes, Colin forces himself to leave it a little longer before asking: 'Has anyone found anything?' Nobody takes any notice of him. After a minute or so, Alan sidles up to him:

ALAN: 'I found a chest.'

COLIN: 'Did you open it?'

ALAN: 'Of course not.'

COLIN: 'Can we open it?'

ALAN: 'Yes, I suppose so.'

COLIN: 'There's a chest here, folks. Shall we open it?'

DAWN: 'What's in it?'

COLIN: 'Come and see. Perhaps there'll be something in it for you. You never know with things you find under water.'

The members of the group prepare to take it in turns to search the contents of the chest, and select something for themselves that would be particularly welcome. Colin stops them.

COLIN: 'Don't choose. Just take what's there. It isn't a choosing chest, it's an accepting chest. Whatever it is, take it.'

When everybody has done this, they stand in a ring, holding on to their gift with their left hand, and their partner with their right one. They close their eyes, while Colin describes the journey back home – leaving the seabed, rising up through water-weed and shoals of fish, past whales and porpoises, to being taken on board a cargo steamer and finally delivered home again. The narrative gains speed and loses detail as the day hospital hall grows nearer.

Back home again, group members subside into chairs – not those along the wall, but a ring of chairs in the place where they have been standing. Colin asks them for memories and experiences.

ALAN: 'It was a bit like being here. Boring.'

COLIN:	'Boring?'
ALAN:	'Mind you, it was OK, on the bottom of the sea...'
COLIN:	'Why?'
ALAN:	'I don't know. I felt I'd reached sea-bottom!'
COLIN:	'Did anybody else feel that?'
RAY:	'A feeling that things couldn't get worse.'
JENNY:	'Yes. It was awful, but it was kind of comforting.'

Dawn and Ken say that they remember feeling the same kind of thing.

COLIN:	'Are you glad you're back, then?'
MAVIS:	'I'm certainly glad I'm back. I hated it down there.'
JENNY:	'Why? What was so awful about it?'
MAVIS:	'It was like being dead. Pointless, futile. Nothing had any reason.'
ANDREW:	'Yes, that's what I felt too.'
MAVIS:	'I couldn't even get anything good from the chest...'

Colin suggests that everybody might like to say what their gifts were. Jenny has a flower, Mavis a coloured stone, Dawn a galleon, Ray a parchment, Ken a crucifix, Andrew a gold coin, and Alan a beetle. Nobody – except Andrew – can think of any real use for what they've got. Perhaps they could invent a use? Colin suggests that they make up a story joining all these objects together. This will help them think of them in a more positive way. When this is over Jenny says:

'I'll keep this [*her flower*] to remind me of what's happened today.'

The idea is taken up with enthusiasm.

RAY:	'We could make up a story about the things we found in the chest at the bottom of the sea. Starting off from here. We could do it for next week.'

On this note the group says goodbye.

This is a liminal session symbolising in embodied form the fruitful chaos which is at the heart of existential change. This is heaven as release from worldly constraints and limitations; heaven as freedom. The use of the imagery of water, natural symbol of both dissolution and renewal, underlines its meaning for everybody present. The stories produced by group members afterwards showed that they had interpreted what had happened in terms of events in which they themselves had been involved at a personal level: they felt changed by the experience. The use of an overall scenario – seaside leading to sea, leading to objects from a sea-chest – made it possible for the pre-liminal phase to act as a kind of introductory symbol of change (seaside – idea of being 'dead or really old' in the hospital – enjoying oneself beside the sea). This is connected to the next group of three sections, the liminal one, by the image of the sea itself, mirrored in action, which leads into the preparations for the voyage (pre-liminal). The voyage itself would be a liminal movement, but it is pre-empted by the storm and 'drowning' which constitute the central chaos of the liminal phase and of the whole session. The post-liminal triad concerns the sea-chest: first, taking the gifts; second, rising to the surface with them; third, making up the story together and writing about them individually.

CHAPTER 5

Rites of Passage
The Voyage to Higher Ground

We have seen that drama, religion and healing are inter-connected. It has been frequently claimed that they spring from the same source. Throughout the world, religion and medicine are bound together in social institution and individual experience, by rituals whose origins are 'lost in the mists of time'. Any investigation of religion, however brief and introductory, must take some account of the healing rituals which mediate a sense of the presence of the divine at a personally transforming level, one which actually increases the physical and psychological well-being of men and women taking part. Physical changes occur as a result of psychological ones; this is religious therapy, not magical rite. There is, in the authentic approach to religious healing, no suggestion that divinity should be manipulated or even cajoled, but simply approached as the expression of human need. The intention here is to express what Mary Douglas has called 'a well-made wish' (1966).

In fact, a good deal of psychological healing depends on how well wishes are made. In psychoanalysis, in behaviour therapy, in dramatherapy, and even in the juxtaposition of chairs in the physician's consulting room, attention is paid to the way an encounter is staged. Events of this kind are presented in ways that affect the participants' sense of the *kind* of reality that he or she must react to in order to respond to a therapist's intentions. Settings can stimulate one's imagination, lull one's fears and anxieties, focus one's attention, make one feel important, remind one of one's place, isolate, include. It would be hard to think of a way of framing an interview that said nothing at all. In fact such a thing would be very disturbing, because we are used to picking up clues from the environment as to how we should behave. Many therapeutic approaches call for a corresponding re-arrangement of personal reality on the part of the patient or client. Simulation, role-play, modelling, Kelleian 'fixed-role therapy' (Kelly, 1955: 360–451) are widely used 'theatrical' approaches, all of which depend on an agreement between client and therapist to explore an alternative inter-personal reality. This agreement is basic to the psychotherapeutic endeavour, which depends on the exploration of alternative ways of being oneself, none of which exist before they have been brought into existence, and none of which will last unless they have been practised. The therapist's world is one of serious make-believe. Apart from which, the client himself is reproducing his or her experience in a particular way and in a contrived setting. As Flowers says, 'The major difficulty in writing about simulation and role playing in psychotherapy and related helping endeavours is that almost all therapy can be viewed as a simulation of the client's real life' (1975: 159).

The action of consciously presenting an emotional reality is always dramatic. Drama itself is 'a frame for action' (Burns, 1972: 17) drawing attention to a particular quality of interpersonal reality, to be perceived in and for itself and its immediate meaning and significance. Actions are framed to draw special attention to them so that they might be studied 'in themselves' and the meaning they are intended to possess may 'stand out' from whatever else is going on (Elam, 1988: Ch. 4). This is the intention behind the dramatic gestures, pauses, tones of voice, vocal inflections that we all use, either deliberately or automatically, to draw attention to the significance of what we are saying or doing. Formal drama, of course, involves the invention of stories and 'characters'; but the process is essentially the same. It is action, experience and intention set at a distance from ordinary communication by a change of presentational tone, a kind of bracketing, which has the general effect of making us concentrate harder and involve ourselves more. This is why, in theatre and ritual, what is less real – more contrived, less natural – is often more effective, more immediately involving, more moving, either to tears or laughter (Grainger, 1990: 17–27).

The historical connection between drama, ritual and healing lies in the fact that all three are ways of construing human experience in terms of story. This is not to say that every healing event or religious experience takes the kind of narrative form that drama itself does. All three, however, are 'makers' of narrative in the sense that, when they occur, they have a story-forming effect on surrounding events: 'And then God spoke to me, and everything began to make sense. I could see what it had all been leading up to...'; 'When I went into hospital I thought it was the end. Now I can see it was a kind of new beginning'; 'It was the last thing I expected, but somehow it seems as if it was inevitable now.' The Bible itself delivers its message in the form of contextual cycles, groups of events that yield meaning when taken together rather than as separate incidents, but which in their entirety present a gigantic cycle from creation to apocalypse, within which is the heroic quest of the Messiah from incarnation to apotheosis. Northrop Frye elaborates the idea by directing attention to the fact that 'Within this again are three other cyclical movements, expressed or implied: individual from birth to salvation; sexual from Adam and Eve to the apocalyptic wedding; social from the giving of the Law to the established kingdom of the law, the rebuilt Zion of the Old Testament and the millenium of the New' (1957: 316, 317). It is not the mythological and historical parts of the Bible which give it its nature as narrative; the cyclic arrangement on which the whole depends for its final meaning carries the imprint of story, just as clearly as the personal testimonies of former hospital patients do when they describe their lives before and after the experience of illness and recovery that changed their way of looking at the world and their evaluation of what happens in it.

In the rite of passage the cyclic narrative takes the form of a healing event. In this chapter we shall be looking at rituals of transformation in the light of the contribution that they make to the therapeutic effect of drama. First, religious ritual registers religious awareness by means of acted symbolism. In rites of passage a religious idea about the emergence of life from death is presented as a dramatic narrative. The combination of idea and presentation makes the event a basic factor of human awareness; a species-characteristic means of ordering the way men and women make sense of existence. The imagery available in religious rituals embodying death and resurrection is of inestimable value for bringing home the vital importance of other changes which take place in the lives of individuals and societies. Because of their reference to infinity, rites of passage are ways of restoring us to our original identity. They reconcile the primal to whatever is to come, allowing us to experience a life renewed and full of possibility. As we might expect from the nature of sacred events, time seems to have been suspended; the experience of things in flux, imperfect and unfinished, is transformed by the access of a perfection able to orient events and give meaning to individual experience. In other words, the rite puts the kind of experience described in the last section into context.

Second, like ritual itself, the rite of passage initiates us into a new kind of being and joins us to those who are already there. It is by being joined to them that we are initiated into newness. This happens in various ways, at various levels of religious significance, but it always has the effect of restoring hope. Patients in the surgical wards of a hospital celebrate the return of a brother or sister from the theatre, by giving thanks in their own individual ways: those who have already 'been down' are a kind of blessed aristocracy, regarding life – and death – quite differently from the rest. 'In baptism you were buried with him, in baptism also you were raised to life with him, through your faith in the active power of God who raised him from the dead' (Colossians, 2: 12). Ritual initiation of this kind constitutes 'A re-enactment of what has occurred in the past, generally to a cult-hero' (Elkin, 1946: 43). The idea of relationship is of fundamental significance. In rite after rite throughout the world the symbolism depends on blood brother or sisterhood in some form or other. The initiand passes through death because he or she participates in the life (and consequently death) of someone who has already done so. Past, present and future are united in the eternal action while time stands still.

This is why the rite is such a special event, taking those who participate into a higher sphere of being. In the original happening which is re-presented here, the divine meaning was communicated in a way which would make it accessible for all times, but in a definitive form. In order to preserve the nature of this particular kind of message, the only kind that really makes sense to human beings, it is constructed out of the fabric of our personal and social lives. This gives the rite of passage a wonderful flexibility, allowing it to act as a universal sign-language without any of the restrictions of spoken and written languages. Here, meaning is acted out according to a scenario which may be used to express any kind of change happening within human life: 'The process of initiation', says Eliade, 'seems to be co-existent with any and every human condition' (1965: 128).

Third, those elements of human experience which make change to a better or higher way of being difficult and painful, are included in the rite of passage within the order of a definite process whose outcome is an experience of union with divine perfection. The process takes the shape of an acted story, which, because it depends on the transmission of an idea about progress by means of movement between different geographical locations, involves a real journey. As we have seen, ritual necessitates the abandonment of private intention for public action. The individual's journey towards higher ground involves him or her in experiences of a painful reality, the symbolic analogues of psychological and sociological factors which are not always clearly identifiable, as well as ones that are. The action of reproducing an individual's journey above and beyond the present in the form of ritual gives him or her a clearer understanding of change and growth as something that really happens, something to be assimilated as experience rather than speculated upon as thought. Because of its use of human actors and the life-like shape of its scenario, the rite shows us change in the nature of personal reality in the form of a social event rather than an abstract idea or aesthetic experience.

As we have seen, one of the ways in which drama and ritual signal their nature as communication of a special privileged reality is by their *shape*, that is, with regard to the order in which events take place. There must, for instance, be some kind of climax, an event which encapsulates the action because the entire story 'pivots' on it. It is the reason for the story; if it did not happen there would be nothing particular to report. There must be a starting point to locate the story in general reality and signal its departure from it: once upon *a time*... There must be a kind of consummation, or again, there is no point to it all. These three things, beginning, climax and ending do not necessarily have to be presented in this order. Thus, part of the skill of telling stories lies in re-arranging the order in which they are told, using technical tricks like 'flash-backs', 'stories-within-stories', 'false climaxes', consciously ambiguous endings. These things 'work' because they do not really fool us. However hard we try the story's innate shape reasserts itself. Indeed the harder we have to try, the more powerful the impact of the story as a real narrative with a beginning, a middle and an end.

Everywhere, it is the triple shape of the rite that brings the reality of message across (Grainger, 1988b). The message is assertive and effective, an experience rather than an idea. Or rather it is an idea in experiential form. Whether it is 'religious' or 'therapeutic' is a pointless question. If it is genuinely the first it will also be the second. Rites of passage are religious in a way that is transforming, renewing, healing. Kilburn and Richardson, writing in the *American Psychologist*, assert that 'Both psychotherapeutic treatment and religious conversion serve certain ritual functions. Renunciation, expiation and cleansing manifest themselves in both contexts' (1984). Successfully treated or converted individuals emerge in a metaphorically transformed sense as individuals re-socialised into a new psychological or social world. They assert that the tripartite shape of such rituals 'impress on the initiate (1) how a change in one's self is sequentially managed within a particular structure with the assistance and guidance of a particular person or group; and (2) how the outcomes can be ultimately attributed to one's own efforts' (1984: 237–251). We have seen that both these factors play a fundamental role in the way that ritual functions. There is the need for a formal structure to separate two kinds of reality, and an identifiable presence able with authority to transform experience; there is the equally important need to feel that what is going on is one's own spiritual journey, representing one's own highest aspirations, a sign of self-transcendence.

Other psychologists have investigated psychotherapeutic approaches based on the model of the rite of passage. In a study of the alcoholics' support association, Syanon, Ofshe and his associates (1974: 66–67) identified several ritual characteristics:

1. An introductory period, which begins the meeting in a low-key way; this led to:

2. A main section of high arousal, characterised by intense emotion. This involved the dramatisation of personal experience, focusing on an individual member of the group, whose story reveals him or her as having somehow, at great odds, triumphed over addiction. The emotional, dramatic presentation, in which all those present are involved, provides a memorable experience, stamping in the reality of actual changes which can and do take place.

3. Those involved 'see life differently' as a result of the heightened experience of the meeting. The notion of self-change is re-asserted in a more hopeful way.

Therapies retain the shape of the rite of passage because it is the inalienable shape of transformation. They reproduce the physical and temporal circum-stances of the rite because these have a specific ability to focus healing. As Sue Jennings says: 'A ritual time and place is set aside for therapeutic interaction' (1987: 15). In this special setting, 'the emphasis is on metalan-guage and subtext'. In other words, even thought and language are special, referential, looking 'beyond' their ordinary, non-ritual application to mean-ings beyond meaning. It is in this kind of setting that real change, 'in depth' change, takes place. Under these circumstances the present is free from the passage of time and the restriction of place, so that it can develop its own possibility. This is the place and time reserved for cutting loose and floating free, a disturbing time, one without precedent, when there is no past and too many alternative futures; the central movement which is timeless and place-less. Perhaps we assume a role – patient, worshipper, therapist, priest – in order to give ourselves something familiar to cling on to; or maybe we identify with a dramatic character, someone in the story, so that we may gain passage through the chaos of alternative possibilities. In such a setting, our usual roles lose their compulsory nature; whereas the roles we have chosen stay with us when the fictional story ends, so that we can find ways of building them into our daily lives. Thus, as Jennings says, 'the drama is both the container of the chaos and the means of exploring it' (1987: 15).

A threshold of experience is approached, arrived at and achieved. The time-scale is not important; it is the journey that matters, not how long it takes. It must be carried out seriously and self-consciously, with the sense of having been properly carried out according to the prescribed form, or it will not have the psychological reality it must possess in order to be a genuine turning point in life. The more painful it is, the more likely we are to pay attention to what it means. This being the case, its pain must be increased. The real pain is inherent in the process of dying and rising again, leaving behind all that is known and loved and trusted, in order to face things that may be quite terrifying and are certainly unknown. In rites of passage this is marked by the violence of experiences contrived to reveal its meaning. Past and future are forgotten, only the present exists for the initiand, who finds him or herself subjected to an apparently endless succession of experiences of a disturbing and even degrading nature. The agony of the passage rite is contrived, as is everything else about it. It is a symbol of the true meaning of life, the consciousness of deliverance celebrated by Viktor Frankl. It is unforgettable, so that the deliverance it heralds may be real.

Some therapeutic approaches consciously reproduce the shape of the rite of passage in order to achieve the same kind of existential transformation. Dramatherapy is one of them. According to Jennings 'As therapists we can accompany our clients on a journey from unwell being to well being' (1987: 13). It will be a journey that depends on imaginative metaphor as much as literal statement, using art to give shape to nature and expressing everything in the language of the ritual movement from 'lower' to 'higher'. Thus tokens can be exchanged, dangers faced, defeats recovered from, metaphysical assistance invoked, all the episodes of a mythical 'hero's journey' towards final deliverance and the fulfilment of his or her fate may be presented in sequence. Dramatherapy both follows the shape and employs the imagery of rite.

Disturbed and anxious people bring their own misery and confusion to the sufferings of the central part. The rite provides a situation specially contrived for containing chaos. Here, of course, the shape of ritual comes into play. By concentrating on the first and last parts of a session in order to establish their identity as 'beginning' and 'ending', a dramatherapist creates a central area in order to explore, with his group, ways of giving shape to the chaotic feelings and perceptions which exist among them. Just as ritual is a way of expressing the reality of religious transformations, so dramatherapy uses the same means, and some of the same ideas, to mediate psycho-spiritual healing.

The rite's healing power subsists largely in its demonstration of something that we would prefer very much to ignore: the real nature of human change. When we think about change we move dyadically from 'before' to 'after' as if there were nothing in between, nothing to link them and maintain psychological continuity. When the change concerned is an important one we would rather be up and away, giving reality to whatever is going to happen than hang about thinking about it. In the state of mind which is neither one thing nor the other we do not know what to think, or how to feel, except uncomfortable. It is only afterwards, when the change has been effectively made, that we appreciate the value of the 'middle section', the seemingly pointless journey between then and now, when we wandered aimlessly about without seeming to get anywhere at all. A. B. Kempe drew attention to the human tendency to think in terms of discrete classes and to pay little heed to the terms of their differentiation (1890).

So far as existential transformation is concerned, the central part of change turns out to be the vital stage. The rite's effectiveness as an instrument of change consists in its ability to realise this stage and overcome our tendency to elide it. In the rite, the facts about human change are articulated within a single event, without any glossing over of the crucial central section which is the psychological reality of change, as distinct from mere wishful thinking. By illustrating the preconditions of a real movement in life, rather than a mental jump, ritual tells us something vitally important about change. In the case of painful changes, those which may affect our happiness or even our health – our position in society, the way we are accustomed to organise our personal worlds, the routines of daily living, the trauma of a loved person's illness or death – we 'think around and ahead' more determinedly than ever.

Thus rites of existential transformation realise the need to change more effectively than merely thinking or talking about it does. Such rites are 'practical blue prints for wished-for states of affairs' (Grainger, 1987: 14) intervening to substitute the language of story for that of argument. The three-fold shape demonstrates the basic qualifications for being any kind of story – the possession of a beginning, a middle and an end. None of these parts may be omitted and the rite retain its message, nor can additions and accretions disguise it. The succession of events brings home a vision of purpose and hope. This is taken hold of to be sanctified. Similarly, place is made more holy and more real through a geographical progression: 'The passage from one social position to another is identified with a territorial passage, such as the entrance into a village or a house, the movement from one room to another, or the crossing of streets and squares' (Hameline, 1972: 112). By presenting its message in the form of an acted story, with a clearly articulated plot and an extended setting; by using ordinary people and locations to act a metaphysical journey; and by treating time in the language of place, the rite participates in the changes to which it points. 'We are not concerned with a ternary scheme or concept of separation, transition and incorporation, but with a demonstrated happening, in which real change is brought about' (ibid.).

From the early days of dramatherapy Sue Jennings has described its action as that of a rite of passage. She has extended the idea in successive books, and often referred to it in seminars and lectures. The analogy is straightforward. Like a rite of passage, dramatherapy is essentially a way of regarding events from a particular view-point, rather than doing things to people in order to change their condition in a direct or instrumental manner. It is a way of handling time in order to give life shape. Because it deals with 'out-of-joint' time, the principle of the rite of passage suggests itself as a way of approaching all kinds of situations of human breakdown, whether physical, emotional or both. Occasions when the network of personal meanings upon which we depend for our identity is no longer able to bear our weight; periods of mental indecision and disorientation, when we do not know which way to turn for help; times of actual illness, when we can no longer hold on to what has been, up to now, a secure part of our universe, whose imminent collapse threatens all the rest – all these and countless others, including the presence of tragic events which leave us helpless and hopeless, can form the subject matter of the confusion at the heart of the rite, the place that is entered and left behind.

Case Study

Tony's childhood was unextraordinary. He had been brought up in a Sheffield suburb during the years following the Second World War. Like so many others in that particular neighbourhood his social life was dominated by school and church. The school was the local grammar school and the church was Methodist. Tony's parents had decided not to send him to boarding school, although they could have afforded to do so. Instead, they kept him at home, for much the same reason that they preferred the Methodist church rather than the Parish church. The family ethos centred around a kind of Puritanism. Protestant standards of morality were easier to maintain at home than away, and this went for religious practices as well. It was a family ethos that had been passed from generation to generation. Tony saw nothing wrong with it, despite the anguish involved in reconciling it – or rather failing to do so – to the emergent sexuality of adolescence. In the early 1960s Tony married a woman with a background similar to his own. The marriage was remarkably free from incident, Tony and Margaret dedicating themselves to preserving the traditional values of middle-class family life and providing a secure background for their twin girls, for whose benefit the pattern of school and chapel was carefully repeated.

Round about the time of the children's sixteenth birthday, Tony's wife left him and them, in order to live with a man she had met at a chapel anniversary dance. It was this domestic catastrophe that was considered to be the cause of the chronic anxiety states he developed over the next 15 years. While the twins were at home he managed to perform adequately as a single parent, although the girls maintain that he was always exceedingly strict and allowed them very little freedom 'even though we were grown up'. This is probably why, as soon as they could manage it, they too left home.

When Tony first came to the day hospital, he was living by himself. One of the twins visited him twice a week. The other had gone abroad. Tony was diagnosed as suffering from anxiety/depression. He was a quiet self-deprecating person. At the level of ordinary social relations he made friends easily enough, partly because of his eagerness to please, or at least not to stand out as being awkward. When asked if he would be willing to join a dramatherapy group, he said he had no objection. Why should he have? It was part of the treatment, after all.

Tony had reason to be grateful for having taken this attitude towards something which, in fact, made him rather nervous. In particular, Tony did not like the idea of exercises involving physical movement. He felt he had little grace and skill and had unhappy memories of school (he was rather overweight). He disliked being made self-conscious, which he certainly did not associate with any kind of psychiatric help he was able to imagine. As he said himself, 'We came here to get better, and you're making us all feel worse.' He was only partly joking. As a matter of fact the remark was more constructive than he knew, an attitude which bound the group together, helping them to overcome their individual uncertainties. It also demonstrated that one could 'be oneself' and still remain within the group, which is the most important thing of all. As dramatherapy employs a lot of movement, Tony had plenty of opportunity to get used to the feel of his own body, something he had never before been encouraged to do. Sessions often began with some kind of exploration of physical experience. On one occasion, vital for Tony's restoration to health, the group were walking about imagining that the floor was a swamp, and that they were all walking through thick, deep mud. They could run and jump in it, or simply stand still and enjoy the squelchy feeling of it between their toes. If they wanted, they could sit down in it, or even roll about, if they liked... Next, they were to imagine it had changed into something else... The same kinds of things were to be done, but the medium was now quite different. After a few moments Tony left the room. He didn't come back until the session was nearly over. People were talking about a mime they had been working on; when Tony started to talk about the mud they were not really interested. The leader, sensing that here was something Tony really wanted to share with the group, asked him what his special material had been.

TONY: 'It felt like ground glass. It didn't hurt, though. You could kick your feet in it as if it were sand. It was strange, though.'

LEADER: 'How? Can you tell us?'

TONY: 'It's a bit silly, really.'

GEOFF (group member): 'That's all right, isn't it?' (*He secures the attention of the rest of the group.*)

TONY: 'The ground glass kept getting clear. Every second or third step it became like a window and you could see things.'

PAT (group member):   'What sort of things?' (*Pause*)

TONY: 'Don't laugh.' (*He is visibly shaken.*)

LEADER: 'Nobody's going to laugh. It was your experience. You tell us.'

TONY: 'Beasts. Monsters.'

GEOFF: 'You mean like a horror movie?'

TONY: 'No, real monsters. But like kid's monsters. There's a book, *Where the Wild Things Are.* Like that. I knew these things; they were horrible...'

Tony was willing to let some of the monsters be presented in mime. He would not take part in this himself, but gave graphic instructions to the group as to size, appearance, way of moving etc. (He even had definite ideas about noise and smell.) As the session proceeded Tony became more involved in what was going on. He never became a 'wild thing' himself, but when the menagerie was complete he took his place in the centre of the action as if he were ringmaster. The creatures began to dance round him making hideous noises. For a moment it was very frightening indeed. Afterwards Tony said he had been terrified. He kept his hands close in at his sides, holding on to the seams of his trousers. Then, suddenly, he lifted his hands over his head and laughed aloud.

When everyone had had enough stamping and shrieking, people subsided to the floor.

TONY: 'I'm sorry.' (*Pause*)

PHILIP (group member): 'We enjoyed it.'

LEADER: 'How are you feeling?'

TONY: 'I've got a headache. I don't want to say anything.'

MARY (group member): 'It was fun. Thanks, Tony. Can I ask you just
            one thing? Did you recognise anyone?'

TONY: 'Oh yes.'

LEADER: 'Perhaps Tony would like to talk, but not yet. Is that right,
            Tony?'

TONY: 'I don't know. Yes. Not yet.'

MARY: 'Well, it was a game. We made it up, didn't we?'

Soon afterwards the session ended, members making sure that Tony wasn't
by himself. The next session was largely led by Tony who wanted to explore
the monsters again and relate them to things about himself and other people.
He said he felt much better: 'Better than I've felt for a long time. Much less
anxious.'

This episode illustrates some of the most important things about the
medium. Most obviously it is an example of the function of dramatherapy
as an aid to *self-disclosure*. As Dorothy Langley has succinctly stated: 'In this
way we see that acting is not a matter of donning a mask and pretending,
but of removing a mask and revealing' (1983: 102). Kicking your feet
through imaginary mud may be just as effective a way of removing your
mask as playing Hamlet is. It is certainly a *bodily state* involving the release
of nervous tension. It is *active* rather than passive, concerned with experiencing the world in an immediate way (at ground level, perhaps!). It happened
within a special kind of social setting, providing the essential *structure* for
therapeutic encounter and imaginative involvement. This could not have
taken place without the complete understanding and acceptance of the group
and the sense of corporate identity which gave courage to each individual
member. A special place, a special time. At this point in Tony's life past,
present and future coincided in an experience of *insight* able to make sense
of an entire personal history: to make it a history rather than the mere
succession of events.

It could be said that this is the real purpose of the medium. It presents us
with a metaphor of life, and so directs attention to the meaning of the things
that happen to us. The structure which we crave is implicit in the metaphor,
but we do not find our personal metaphor easily. It is hard to appreciate the
outline of even that part of the forest we know well. When we climb a tree

we can see very little apart from more trees, and the unfathomable sky. We need some way of lifting ourselves up above the place we know so we may catch a glimpse of what the forest really is, where it stretches from and reaches to. We all need this, but some are more claustrophobic than others.

CHAPTER 6

The Hero's (Heroine's) Journey

For the dramatherapeutic metaphors considered up to now the dramatherapy session is a way of entering an ideal form of reality. To take part in such a session is to be conformed to the life and death of a saving (i.e. healing, transforming) person – for example the group leader in the first session described, who led the group 'back to the surface' by getting them to put their trust in him. Because dramatherapy sessions always obey roughly similar rules, involving a special privileged place, where one is led by someone acknowledged as in charge, there is always a powerful element of conformity. What is happening is exemplary and, metaphorically speaking, typical.

In the 'Hero's Journey' the emphasis changes to individual action. Because many versions of this are based on well-known myths, and have at one or other level of consciousness actual religious authority, the element of exemplarism is still very strong. Even stronger, however, is the sense of personal adventure, the discovery of new life through one's own initiative. This metaphor is concerned with solving problems through experience; with the way things 'fall into place' once the 'whole picture' is taken into account. For this approach true understanding depends on hindsight, because 'the quality of a given event is its intuited wholeness or total character' (Pepper, 1942: 238). Meaning for the hero is located in his or her continuing sense that all will be revealed at journey's end, and that at any particular time until then, truth is in the making. As far as human beings are concerned, heaven is a process rather than a place, and cannot be understood properly now because it is not finished. Kierkegaard's remark, that 'Life is lived in the future and understood in the past' could be taken as a slogan for the hero/heroine's journey.

Dramatherapy based on mythology often takes the form of an epic journey of some kind. In many, perhaps even most, myths, the emphasis is upon the story itself rather than its ending, and the story is always a kind of journey, even if the hero or heroine never leaves home. In the typical hero's journey, however, this spiritual journey is acted through, in progression from place to place, adventure to adventure. The spiritual significance of this kind of progression is brought home by the fact that it occurs times without number in the religious experience of mankind. This is not the same thing as the use of geographical location to express a particular kind of socio-religious progression for initiatory purposes, as in a rite of passage. For all its extended threefold shape this signifies a single event rather than a process – although it is, of course, a process. Rites of passage are based upon religious mythology of this kind, and their identity as story is essential to their power as symbols of transformation. All the same, they possess the ability to hold events together around a central pivotal point in order to constitute one single dramatic event. The hero's journey of religious mythology is a much more extended affair than this. Examples are to be found in almost every religion, if not in its official theology then in the folk lore which surrounds it and the popular forms deriving from it. Joseph Campbell's work has drawn attention to its universality as a religious archetype: 'Hero ventures forth from the world of common day into a region of supernatural wonder: fabulous forces are there encountered and a decisive victory is won: the hero comes back from this mysterious adventure with the power to bestow boons on his fellow man' (1988: 30).

The story-telling which is a vital part of dramatherapy models itself on epic stories of this kind, either directly or by means of extemporised narratives which obey the same structural rules. Religious myth at its simplest conforms to an obvious pattern: a person or group of people journey away from home towards an unknown place, where different kinds of danger lie in wait. Because it is unknown territory, anything could happen here, and it is impossible for travellers to be completely prepared. There are many adventures, but finally the hero or heroes return. The return signifies not only the end of the ordeal undergone by the person or persons who have been away, it is taken as a kind of deliverance by those left at home. What this consists of – whether it is merely relief from anxiety as to the fate of a loved person, or whether the journey brings back deliverance in the form of some kind of spiritual enrichment – depends on whatever version of the story it might be. I have pointed out elsewhere that this kind of imaginative experience has a very definite therapeutic effect: 'Conducting us away from our habitual frames of reference, loosening our construct systems and breaking down the fixed patterns of neurotic thinking with the permeability of the symbolic narrative' (Grainger, 1990: 126). By 'permeability', I mean the way in which the story lends itself to so many interpretations while retaining its identity as an expression of purpose and meaning in human life. Throughout the world this basic story form makes religions practical by giving people a kind of luminous clue as to the relationship between spiritual awareness and life. It conveys a sense of *possibility* that no abstract philosophy or systematic theology can achieve. The fact that it shares this sense of possibility is perhaps the single most spiritual thing about dramatherapy.

In most cases the myth of the journey is more extended. This has the effect of concentrating attention on journey as process rather than event (although, of course, as far as its overall significance is concerned it is certainly both). Here are two examples. The first is the 'Saving Acts' of Christ. These are summed up in terms of one single action, whereby Christ 'died for our eternal redemption' (Hebrews, 9: 12). The description as to how this came about, however, constitutes the account of an extended journey recorded in the gospels – a journey through time to eternity, taking place in nine stages from the Garden of Gethsemane to the Ascension, via Crucifixion, descent into Hell, and Resurrection. Seen in terms of the hero's journey, the central structural element is not the Cross, the 'shattering of the gates of Hell', but Hell itself: chaos, the descent into un-being. The Cross is the means whereby this is achieved. The entire journey 'from death to life' is divisible into nine sections, each of which falls naturally into a rite of passage, but which all together make up an extended narrative or 'saving history'. The first triad – Gethsemane, the Trial of Jesus, Pilate's sentencing, are linked together by the theme of suffering and betrayal typified by the image of the eternal Word cross-examined by a Roman official. After this a link passage, the carrying of the cross, leads from the sentence of crucifixion to Crucifixion itself. This central triad involves the death of Christ, his sojourn in hell, and his resurrection from death. This is dramatically expressed in the empty tomb, itself divided from the Ascension by the tantalising mixture of reassurance and frustration, the emotional chaos of the Resurrection appearances. The complete journey is as follows:

	Pre-liminal		*Liminal*		*Post-liminal*
Pre-liminal	Gethsemane	→	Trial	→	Sentencing
Liminal	Crucifixion	→	Descent into hell	→	Resurrection
Post-liminal	Empty tomb	→	Resurrection appearances	→	Ascension

Figure 6.1. Christ's Easter Journey

The Easter narrative is the central part of a longer story which begins with Jesus's own ministry and ends with the Acts of the Apostles. Its shape corresponds to that of many religious myths and imaginative stories throughout the world. This should not be interpreted to mean that it is in any important sense untrue. This is the way that we record all our really important insights about the nature of life. The more perfect our conviction, the more certain we are to enshrine it in threefold form, what Euclid described as 'The shape of perfection'.

This is strikingly demonstrated in the second example: the central myth of Buddhism. The Hero prince Gautama (Campbell, 1988; 192) sets forth in secret from his father's closely guarded palace under the protection of 60,000 divinities, and vaults across an immensely wide river. He cuts off all his hair, except for one strand, and wanders through the world as a mendicant monk. During these years of aimless wandering he masters the eight stages of meditation, a task that, because of the extreme asceticism involved, brings him to the threshold of death. He recovers, however, and continues his wandering. One day, sitting under a tree and gazing eastwards, he is approached by a young girl, Sujata, who offers him a golden bowl of rice. He eats and tosses the bowl into a river flowing by. The golden bowl floats up-stream – a sign of his approaching Buddha-hood. He rises and proceeds along an immensely broad road, animals, birds and flowers rising to do him homage as he passes by, the heavens full of music and heavenly singing, all nature pouring out its richness of scent, sound and colour. And so he reaches the Tree of Enlightenment, the place of the universe's redemption, and sits down on the Immovable Spot.

Kama-Mara, god of love and death, mounted on his elephant and surrounded by an army, hurls all kinds of weapons and missiles against him, as well as whirlwinds, boiling mud, burning coal etc., but he turns everything into flowers and ointments. Kama-Mara's seductive daughters are no more successful than his warriors. Kama-Mara accuses him of trespassing on the Immovable Spot, but the Earth goddess vindicates him. During the night he acquires knowledge of his own previous existences (First Watch), divine vision (Second Watch), and knowledge of the chain of causation (Third Watch). At daybreak he achieves perfect enlightenment. Having become Buddha, the Enlightened, he passes seven periods of seven days. (Remaining motionless, standing aside and gazing at the spot on which enlightenment has come, pacing from the place where he stands to the spot itself, meditating on causality and enlightenment, sitting under the tree where Sujata has brought the bowl and meditating on Nirvana, sheltering from an immense storm under a third tree, and enjoying the sweetness of liberation under a fourth one.) A period of doubt ensues as to whether what he has discovered can be effectively passed on, but Brahma comes to him to beg him to teach humanity the way of enlightenment.

The story falls naturally into three sections. First there is one in which Prince Gautama leaves home and wanders until he arrives at the first tree. The liminal phase takes him beneath the second tree. This is the section of the story introduced by the contest with the god of love and death and describing Gautama's real testing during the three watches of the night, the crucial transformation into Buddha-hood. The post-liminal phase continues to the end of the story. Each of these phases is itself threefold; Gautama's setting forth, his wandering and sickness, his revival (pre-liminal); the liminal, consisting of the battle with Kama-Mara, the intellectual-spiritual struggle for enlightenment, the achievement of enlightenment; the sevenfold ritualisation of the event that has occurred, the period of doubt about the communicability of his message, and Brahma's authentification of it (post-liminal).

	Pre-liminal		*Liminal*		*Post-liminal*
Pre-liminal	Setting forth	→	Kama-Mara	→	Seven-fold rite
Liminal	Wandering/sickness	→	Finding enlightenment	→	Doubting
Post-liminal	Revival	→	Achievement of enlightenment	→	Brahma's validation

Figure 6.2. The Journey of the Buddha

Such is the spiritual power of the hero's journey, its ability to carry the imagination to a higher plane by means of the ordinary processes of identification with the characters of fiction – particularly when those characters arouse our sympathy and involve us first in their trials and then in their triumphs – that any narrative which is authentically fictional will have a spiritual impact. In other words it will possess the wherewithal to tell a real story.

The mythology of the world is full of real stories, with the power to involve and influence us. This is because however fantastic their view-point is, they are still human. They speak about fantasy in our language, that of the emotions and ideas, longings and hopes, strengths and vulnerabilities that we have. They have to do this in order to make sense to us, so that they can carry us along with them. Where they go, we go too. The stories that follow possess this kind of fascination. Apart from dealing with recognisable personal identities, they follow the shape of personal meaning, the order of events which makes up the human unit of experiential sense and permits the event of spiritual change.

A good example is the Hindu myth of Muchukunda, summarised here:

> An ancient Hindu warrior king is born from his father's left side and grows up to have great power, so much so that the gods seek his assistance against the demons, whom he defeats. As a reward, the gods promise to grant him anything he wishes. Because he is so weary, he asks for endless sleep, and retires to a cave to sleep for ever. Anyone who disturbs him will be burned to death by a glance of his eye. Vishnu-Krishna, the incarnate lord of the world, tricks a barbarian king into entering the cave. The intruder kicks the sleeper into life and is burned into a heap of ashes. This leads the sleeper to take refuge with Krishna, being convinced by the heap of ashes of the futility of human solutions, including his own. Leaving the cave he discovers that he has become a giant. He retreats to the highest mountain and dedicates himself to the search for enlightenment.

Clearly, this is a myth of spiritual transformation. Its message is plain. Enlightenment is not to be regarded as a way of leaving the world because of its difficulties and hardships. No humanly devised escape route is possible; there is no way out, only a way *through*. The story is strikingly expressive of change, strenuous activity being followed by exhaustion, enlightenment proceeding from the ashes of the past. The action of the drama concentrates on time rather than space, centred upon a single image of life out of death, the warrior's cave. Through the tomb which is also a womb, the exhausted king becomes the spiritual giant on his way to enlightenment. A myth such as this is open to interpretation at other levels of analysis. The story as presented, however, does not depend on analytical skill, either psychological or theological. It delivers its message simply via its identity as a story. Basically, it is a story about somebody who enters a cave and comes out much later in a transformed condition. This is the event it celebrates. The rest is detail; pregnant detail, certainly, but detail all the same, and not to be allowed to get in the way of the principal statement, which is spiritual rather than psychological. Its spiritual identity and purpose requires the preservation of the narrative in its integrated form as a story with a beginning, a middle and an end, a metaphor of departure, journey and arrival, rather than a collection of symbols related to one another because they occur within a narrative framework. The most potent symbol of the narrative is its identity as narrative – a way of presenting experience which is to be taken whole and not reduced to fragments. The narrative's meta-message is clear: *I am a story*, it says. *Listen to me and get my point.*

Other myths present change by means of a horizontal rather than a vertical metaphor, although there is always an element of both dimensions in their imagery – journeying always involves either the passage of time or its miraculous suspension, sojourning always takes place somewhere or other, either 'in' the world, or 'out' of it. Myths concentrating on a geographical passage resemble the 'hero's journey'.

The following is a story from North America (Navaho):

> Two warriors, feeling homesick, set out for the house of their father, the Sun, not knowing how to get there. They see smoke rising from the ground, and climb down a ladder into the Spider Woman's chamber. Hearing of their difficulty, she warns them of the dangers on the way to the Sun's house. There are four main hazards: crushing rocks, cutting reeds, tearing cacti and boiling sands. The Spider Woman gives them a charm consisting of feathers plucked from a living eagle, and a magic formula, able to lay out a path before them. The two warriors make their way between the rocks, through the reeds and the cactus plants, across the boiling sands, to the magnificent house of the Sun, where they are hidden away by the Sun's children. The Sun, however, has seen them enter, and demands to know who they are. He puts them through a series of strenuous physical trials, culminating in one in which they have to smoke a poisoned pipe. With the help of their magic feathers and the Spider Woman's formula, as well as advice given by friendly animals, the two warriors manage to survive unscathed, and so receive the approbation of their father, the Sun, who says he is proud of them, and grants them all their wishes.

This is a good example of the kind of narrative which occurs all over the world in the form of religious myth, folklore, children's tales (e.g. the Brothers Grimm, Hans Andersen), legends. Such stories are characterised by certain distinctive features, in addition to their basic shape as stories. They begin with the statement of a problem or a purpose. The protagonist is looking for help or relief. In the course of searching for this he/she encounters a personage who offers to help him/her. This may be in exchange for some service carried out, or promised by, the protagonist, and the help may consist of vital information, magical intervention, faithful companionship, etc. A journey is to be undertaken that will involve certain trials and hardships which, if successfully overcome, will bring the protagonist to the heart of his or her problems, the central difficulty in the way of achieving a successful outcome. This is the period of confusion and bafflement, in which the protagonist is totally out-faced, and his or her ability to make sense of what is happening proves inadequate. The key to the situation lies in the assistance provided by the personage he or she encountered on first setting out. A talisman, the words of a rune, a particular ability granted by the personage (such as the ability to fly or to talk to animals) provides a way out of chaos, and the protagonist's problem is solved, whatever it may have been. Usually it has some direct reference to the agony just endured, in some way enabling the agony to make sense. In other words it is the solution not only of the original problem but also of the entire journey of life. The two sons in the Navaho myth have won their father's approval by learning an unlearnable truth. This is one that is only learned in the living of it. Loving father and harsh taskmaster turn out to be the same person, seen from a different point in the journey... Through their encounter with the helper they are given both problem and solution; it is important that the helper is met first *before* the crisis!

The similarity between initiation ritual and 'hero's journey' myth is striking. For instance, the Navaho myth just quoted works out as follows:

A. *Pre-liminal*	*Pre-liminal*	*Liminal*	*Post-liminal*
	Spider Woman – warning and help	Dangers on way to house of the Sun	Entry to house, greeting by Sun
B. *Liminal*	Sun challenges their identity	Trials and tests, poisoned pipe	Survival, with Spider Woman's feather and formula
C. *Post-liminal*----------------Sun's acceptance---			

Figure 6.3. *The shape of the Navaho initiatory myth*

Because this is the story of a journey, the final movement is not unnecessarily developed. The story ends at the natural place, with the arrival at the destination, in this case the Navaho warriors' acceptance by their father. We do not need to know the pre-liminality, liminality and post-liminality of that event, which can stand by itself. Many, but not all, adventure myths end like this.

An example of a threefold ending occurs in the following Irish story:

> In order to heal the queen, the prince sets out to get three bottles of
> water from the flaming well of the fairies. A fairy aunt gives him advice
> and a bedraggled horse to ride on. Mounted on the horse he crosses
> a river of fire and penetrates the poison grove surrounding the
> impregnable castle. The horse shoots over the castle, and the prince
> vaults through the window, to land amid an army of sleeping giants
> and monsters. Passing through these he is confronted with the most
> disturbing situation of all – 12 chambers, each of which contains a
> woman more beautiful than the last, all of them more beautiful than
> he has ever seen in his life. Nevertheless, he resists the impulse to
> disturb their sleep. In the thirteenth room a golden coach moves round
> in a circle, carrying in it the most beautiful woman of all, who
> welcomes him into her coach, where he rests for six days and nights.
> Leaving her, he fills three bottles from the well, writes a letter to the
> queen admitting who he is and what he has done, and climbs on to
> the little horse and goes home, passing safely through the grove and
> over the river.

The filling of the bottles, the letter and the final journey home constitute the
story's post-liminal phase, extended in this case because of the structural
importance of the 'queen in the golden coach', who might well appear to be
the goal of the prince's quest, but is really the post-liminal climax to the
myth's central, liminal, part. The quest ends with the achievement of its
original purpose, the securing and bringing back of the water – hence the
elaboration of the last movement. This element of flexibility at the end of
the story, in which the form is adapted to suit the content, is one of the ways
in which myth differs from rite.

As a symbol of perfection, rite is always symmetrical. Myth, on the other
hand, is a story about human achievement, albeit with supernatural assistance. It is goal-orientated, uni-directional and consequently lop-sided,
having a very definite bias towards the outcome. We have seen that ritual
possesses a unitary quality, and is recorded as an event in three parts rather
than three connected events. Because it refers to a particular privileged area
of human experience, it escapes the ordinary contextual restraints of day-to-
day living, our awareness of the meaningful relationship of events within the
passage of time. Because of the rite's central, pivotal, movement, 'before' and
'after' are not intended to be connected as cause and effect, only as elements
in a supernatural happening. This is not the case with myth, which, despite
its underlying structural similarity to rite is different from it in important

ways. Whereas rite is first and foremost an event, myth is story. The first works by the actual participation of persons in relationship with one another, the second by the use of the imagination to create a personal world 'within' the individual awareness. Drama links them together, opening rite up by giving it the availability and temporal extension, the life-like quality of story, and realising story in the movements, gestures and voices of real people, who present the action with all the seriousness and individual commitment of devotees.

Both rite and myth revolve around radical change. In rite this typically involves a death. Myths of change, however, are more likely to concentrate on ordeals and tests of strength, ingenuity or endurance; the hero/heroine changes as a result of the things he or she has experienced. This is strength through overcoming. At the same time, however, he or she does not have to survive alone, supernatural help being given at crucial points along the way, and also in the social conflict itself. Thus, the human, in co-operation with the divine, pits its wits against whatever power, or powers, hinders its progress, and change is envisaged as growth, development, expression, self-realisation. The aim is not so much divinisation, but a more complete partnership with god or the gods.

It has been said that rite belongs to religion, but myth to literature – spiritual literature, the kind of writing to be found in the *Divine Comedy*, *Paradise Lost* and *The Pilgrim's Progress*. The combination of ordinary naturalistic detail and ideas concerning the underlying or overarching providence of God is reminiscent of a tradition of writing of a non-narrative kind, such as Confucius's Analects, or the eighteenth-century Jesuit confessors; but the kind of literature which actually makes use of myth as an artform is romance. This is the literature of wish-fulfilment, that inhabits a landscape of people, place and events chosen partly for allegorical meaning and partly for symbolic resonance, whose heroes and heroines overcome a succession of obstacles on their way to their visionary meeting with God, but are never really in any danger because of the dream-like nature of what is taking place. 'Romance', says Northrop Frye, 'is naturally a sequential and processional form' whose 'essential element of plot is adventure' (1957: 186). In fact, myth itself is an expansion and exploration of the central movement of the rite, the original 'dream-time' or *alcheringa*, in which the hero/heroine takes on the strength of his or her divine ally and seeks out the enemy instead of being sought out by him. According to Northrop Frye, it 'accounts for and makes communicable the ritual and the dream'. In fact, ritual and dream are already united by the shape of the rite itself, so that all that is needed for romance is to give narrative extent to the moment of change in the rite, thus

making it both safe and communicable, setting it at a distance and giving it
a recognisable literary form. Thus, myth functions to explain ritual, which
makes it less terrifying. The rite, as Frye rightly says, 'cannot account for
itself: it is pre-logical, pre-verbal, and in a sense pre-human' (1957: 102).

Romance certainly makes religion human. It could be said that by blurring
the distinction between fantasy and reality, it makes it too human. At least,
it enshrines the idea of an achievable perfection. The dream here is of a
practical heaven, one which it is both worthwhile and exciting to strive after.
It is the excitement of the quest that keeps us pressing onwards. If the way
is hard, that is what we were expecting. If it turns out to be too hard, even
that can be somehow included in the story.

The therapeutic implications of this journey are quite clear. Our own
adventure-story provides us with a past, a present and a future which are *ours*.
Karl Schäbe suggests that 'The form of human activity known as adventure
has a central role to play in the construction and development of life stories'
(1986: 130). At the very beginning of their investigations into human
behaviour and the experience it embodies, psychologists are confronted with
the necessity to take account of the sheer historicity of personhood. Whether
the past is seen in terms of 'reinforcement history', 'stages of cognitive
development' or the 'resolution of instinctual vicissitudes', we take it on
board as personal ballast for our voyage through life. The things that have
happened to us give us our reality as people because they enable us to stand
back from ourselves and see ourselves in action in the world. It is *then* that
we perceive ourselves, not *now*, for by the time we have drawn our conclusions
about the present, it is the past. Certainly we can look forward, guessing and
hoping, perhaps believing, and this gives substance to the present moment;
but it does so only by referring to what is already experienced, already a part
of the self. It is this 'story of myself' that provides the basis of personhood,
an existential platform for self-possession in the present and personal action
in the future. Someone without this sense of story is like Chamisso's Peter
Schlemihl, the man who lost his shadow (1957). A shadow reflects solidity
and defines shape. My story, like my shadow, is convincing evidence of my
existence, an objective proof of an elusive presence. My shadow is my own;
though I can never pin it down, it reminds me inescapably of my three-dimensional, factual, embodied self, the self that moves in the general world
of men and women. Intangible in itself, my shadow gives me a recognisable
shape.

One of the functions – a primary one – of dramatherapy is to provide a
recognisable background for people whose lives have been disrupted by the
breakdown of vital relationships: people with formless stories and shapeless

shadows. If my story is the way I organise myself as a person among people, the narrative organisation of experience, then practice in organising my story of myself will strengthen my sense of being a person. Dramatherapy provides an ideal medium for this. To be allowed to be hero or heroine of our own adventure is to work personally within the framework of our own story-telling, reminding ourselves of motive and circumstance, sorrow and joy, happiness and grief, expansive response and defensive retraction, seeing these things as important structural factors in the creation of our own unique story, our 'hero's journey' through life. The truth of such a story lies in its making, as the coherence and meaning we give it become our personal coherence and meaning, our personal truth. We do not need to invent episodes in which we behave particularly well in order to feel better. The secret lies in the way we organise the material that is already to hand; the meaning achieved by the process of giving shape and purpose to a disconnected succession of events, and then living them out in dramatic form. We become identified with our story in the process of making it our own.

The original state of confusion does not prevent shape and meaning from emerging. Quite the opposite. George Kelly has drawn attention to a 'creativity cycle' which 'starts with loosened construction and terminates with tightened and validated constructions'. Dramatherapy is an 'agent of validated construction' (1955: 528). Indeed, the aim of art is always to give form to chaos, definition and identity to a moment or relationship of moments within the flux of events. This is the kind of artistic ability we all possess, and that we use to distinguish among the various functional conventions involving multiple role-playing in a hyper-organised society; the kind of thing people mean when they talk about 'getting their act together'. The fact is that we cannot always keep our grasp on what is happening to us, particularly in the face of traumatic changes in our personal lives. At such times things are *too* real for us, too close for comfort. If we are not to retire into ourselves and pretend that nothing is happening we must find a way of standing back in order to assert a kind of control: *reculer pour mieux sauter*, as they say in France. A function of art is to enable us to limit this immediate intuitive involvement by reinforcing the ways in which we naturally make sense of whatever is happening, by structuring events in order to come to terms with them. (In other words, art is the definition of 'It' which draws attention to 'Thou'.)

It is as if our stories have to be edited in order to be our stories. To find our sense we need to know what to look at. The opportunity to use our own creative skill in organising the things that happen to us helps us to make more sense of ourselves as people, by establishing *which* people we in fact

are: 'I need to remember my stories', says James Hillman,[1] 'not because I need
to find out about myself, but because I need to found myself in a story I can
hold to be mine' (1983: 42). (Perhaps this accounts for the appeal of
soap-operas?) In dramatherapy this action of identification-by-location is
embodied in an imaginative interpersonal experience, so that the emerging
narrative is lived out and ideas are actual events. This may provide a stable
experience in a shifting sea of fears and uncertainties, a time when, for once,
things hang together and the chaotic world makes a kind of sense.

(It may be suggested that this kind of approach is also used by explicit
religion nowadays. A more adventurous attitude towards liturgy has made it
possible for worshippers to experience their own spiritual journey in dramatic form, certainly in some Christian congregations, probably in other
religious settings also. Confirmation classes concentrate on the aspect of a
personal history which is validated by reference to a divine hero.)

The Session

Angela (30), Karen (30), Sian (45), Drew (42), Gareth (32), Phil (40), Dick
(50), Terry (30) (Leader). The session takes place in a large activities room
in an Acute Ward at a psychiatric hospital. The group have been working
together for several weeks, taking part in a graded course of sessions. They
have all been diagnosed as suffering from anxiety/depression, although
Gareth shows signs of thought disorder.

As soon as Terry comes in, Angela, Karen and Sian get up and come over
to him. They are keen to start this week's session. Karen says that the last
session was 'great', and wants to know what's going to happen this morning.
The men are not quite so eager, although they join the group round Terry,
and soon begin to show some interest. Terry starts the session by asking the
group to stand in a ring and put their arms round one another's shoulders.
The women are quite happy to do this, the men not so happy, until the order
in which they are standing is revised, and they can have one of their arms
round a woman's neck rather than having to embrace two men. This causes
a certain relaxation of tension. (Angela: 'Would you credit it?') The group

---

1   Hillman sees mythology as a pre-scientific form of psychology, rather than an art form
    requiring psychological analysis or interpretation: 'Psychology is a mythology of
    modernity. The ancients had no psychology, properly speaking, but they had myths, the
    speculative tellings about humans in relation to more-than-human forces and images. We
    moderns have no mythology, properly speaking, but we have psychological systems, the
    speculative theories about humans in relation with more than human forces and images,
    today called fields, instincts, drives, complexes' (1979: 23–24).

sways from side to side. Finding they can sway quite a distance holding one another like this, they try it on one leg, which is more difficult, and they eventually fall over. By now the tension has gone, and the group spend some moments 'grooming' one another, moving round in a circle, each one massaging the back of the person in front as if they were mapping out a jungle road – clearing the way through trees, levelling the ground, laying the paving and asphalt and marking out a white line down the centre. Everybody seems to enjoy this except Gareth, who simply walks round, without touching Sian's back, to her evident annoyance.

TERRY: 'Don't you want to massage Sian's back, Gareth?'

GARETH: 'I don't mind. But not like that!...'

SIAN: 'Go on, make me feel it!'

GARETH: 'OK' (*but he doesn't*).

Terry asks the group if anybody can remember what happened in last week's session. Phil says that it was something about going on a journey. Karen, who hasn't spoken for some minutes, says 'We wrote about someone who was going on a quest. A quest through life. We wrote stories about it. I've still got mine.'

Terry reminds the group about the folk-tale he told them last week.

GARETH: 'We moved round the room climbing over chairs and
           pushing through things. It was OK'

TERRY: 'What was it about, though?'

PHIL: 'About the story. You told us about the river and the forest
           and the swamp, and we did it.'

SIAN: 'And the mountain with the talking unicorn.'

DICK (*after a pause*):   'It was about a hero.'

TERRY: 'Can anyone remember any more than that?'

Slowly the group put together the account of the 'hero's journey' that they worked on last week. They talked about this for almost half the session, so he is surprised at their slowness in responding today. However this turns out to be because the subject proved too interesting rather than not interesting enough. People feel that they have something to contribute, but are not quite sure what it is or how to organise it into words. Terry suggests that they spend this session working on the idea of people's journey through life. Gareth unexpectedly says 'OK'. Terry asks him if he has any suggestions, and he asks if they can use the room, instead of simply talking.

GARETH: 'We can use it to move about in. Not people's backs, the
           room itself.'

Terry asks what would be the best way of doing it. People come up with
various suggestions about this. Sian mentions 'the person who tells him how
to get there'. Phil says 'at one point he meets a dragon, or a giant, and nearly
gets killed'. Angela says, 'that's right, but she has to go through all kinds of
things before she gets that far'.

DREW: 'It's "he" not "she".'

ANGELA: 'Suit yourself.'

DREW (*to Terry*):   'Which is it'

TERRY: 'It depends, doesn't it? "He" for you, "she" for her.'

KAREN: 'Obviously.'

GARETH: 'She or he has a special what d'you call it?'

PHIL: 'It's a talisman. Like this.' (*He shows them the rabbit's foot
           attached to his key chain.*)

TERRY: 'There you are then. What happens next?'

There is a pause. Nobody seems able to answer this. Eventually Phil says:
'Well, that's it, isn't it? You've got there, haven't you?'

DREW: 'It's home.'

ANGELA: 'Well, not quite home, is it? I mean, it's *better* than home
           really.'

SIAN: 'It's the place you set out to get to.'

TERRY: 'So what would you do? To show you're pleased to be there,
           Gareth?'

GARETH: 'Celebrate!'

Everyone agrees. They set out the room to represent the plan of the journey,
marking off the stages identified by the group. The group moves very slowly
from one stage to another, thinking quietly about events in their own lives
that the journey brings to mind. They do this individually, spending as much
time as they want to at each stage. Nobody gets any further than the main
area of conflict, and Angela and Gareth only reach stage two, where they get
stuck. Terry asks if anyone would like to move through as many stages as he
or she can, and say just a few words about the kind of thing they are
remembering as they move along. Drew says he 'doesn't mind', and Phil
begins to say something and stops. Terry looks at him in a questioning way,
but he shakes his head.

DREW: 'I can only get as far as the middle.'

TERRY: 'That's all right. I don't think anyone can get any further than that. Let's put a bench in the middle, shall we, so that we can have a rest when we get there. Off you go, then. Say something about each stage, beginning where you started.'

Drew starts off by describing his fears and hopes as a child, and moves on to his marriage, which gave him a sense of direction and the courage to deal with a succession of problems. His crisis came when his wife left him. Since then he has felt that life has no purpose. He sits on the bench, obviously moved by talking about these things. By now, Phil has made up his mind to undertake the journey. Friendship with a games teacher led to hard-won skill in games, all of which has proved pointless in the light of a road accident and consequent nervous collapse. Phil joins Drew on the bench, which soon holds Karen, Sian and Dick as well. Karen delays her journey by showing what led up to her starting out on it. She is the only one to include this introductory process, which has a definite beginning, middle and end. Nobody was given instructions to prepare in this way.

TERRY: 'What's the first part of the journey about?'

SIAN: 'Getting through things.'

TERRY: 'Yes. How?'

SIAN: 'Someone helps you'. (*Getting the point.*) 'Come on, you two.' (*She takes Angela and Gareth by the hand, and leads them to the bench.*) 'Although I don't know what I'm leading you to.' (*To Terry*): 'What do we do now?'

PHIL: 'He's going to say it's up to us, aren't you?'

TERRY: 'Yes. It's up to you. You've all got something to get you through, something positive that you bring with you from the past. You've all managed to get this far. Take your time.'

DREW *(after a pause)*:   'It's not easy.'

TERRY: 'Well, would you like to stop and do something else? Something easier? All you have to do is to get up off the bench and walk to the other side.'

SIAN: 'Can we close our minds and do it?'

TERRY: 'Just do it.'

SIAN: 'Right.' (*She takes a few steps.*) 'You're wrong. It's not easy.'

Karen goes to her, puts her arm round her shoulder and takes her to the other side. Phil strolls across after her. They hug one another delightedly. Dick strides purposefully across, then turns back to fetch Gareth, who smiles and holds out his hand to Angela. Drew is last to come: 'I don't really think I can face it.' 'Never mind, you came.'

The group hold hands and makes the journey across the room together, pausing at each stage to exchange hugs and handshakes. They end by standing in a circle, their arms around one another's shoulders, as at the beginning. The circle sways and breaks. Everybody says goodbye. They will have an opportunity to do this again if they want.

CHAPTER 7

Creation
The Work of Art

Associated with the experience of self-discovery induced by the dramatherapeutic approach is a perception of the world itself as emerging in a new form, its spiritual significance revealed as an alternative way of interpreting life, and yet as its true meaning. It is as if things were involved in a process of renewal from within, drawing from a primal source of being: the awareness of which renders our customary ways of making sense largely irrelevant. Such an interpretation corresponds to an idea of 'organic wholeness' according to which 'Every element of an organic whole implies every other' (Pepper, 1942: 280). In other words, things do not belong together because meaning arises from the things that happen to them, but simply because they belong together and are 'intended' to be together. In theological terms, they *co-inhere*. This is a global rather than a linear perception, and largely defies description. At least it cannot be described in terms of a simple journey from here to there; but just as there is meaning in the idea of a journey through life, of dangers survived and defeat transformed into victory, so there is meaning in the idea of personal change through homologisation with a pre-existent wholeness, the perfection that was before time began.

Indeed, the meaning of the rite's crucial journey subsists in its nature as 'the shape of a perfect change'. It is an achieved balance, brought about in the nature of human life by the action of eternity. It is the result of a project undertaken to change the nature of reality, both for individuals and societies. We have seen how the rite is always the way of bringing the neophyte into a superior position, one that is socially and spiritually advanced, by means of a process or re-making through a transforming contact with divinity. Socio-religiously speaking, he or she is never the same again, having undergone an essential change. All the same, life in the world is resumed; it is seen from a different viewpoint, but it is the same world. It is the individual and/or the group that has been changed, and changed *actively*. One might almost say systematically – certainly in accordance with definite procedures and a well-formulated intention demonstrated in terms of bodily action and geographical progression.

Spiritual change does not have to be expressed in so active a metaphor, giving rise to such well-defined procedures. The image of the rose or the lotus is as open to religious interpretation as that of road, river, forest, cave and mountain. The message enshrined in examples of perfection, whether they be flowers, animals or people is altogether different from the acted paradigm of the rite of passage. The aim here is to express balance, beauty and repose – the way we believe things would be if we could only discipline ourselves to leave them alone. Human effort plays as large a part in simply realising the rose as it does in sojourning for so many days in the belly of the sea monster. Generally speaking, we find it almost as hard not doing things as either doing them or having them done to us. This is religion as meditation and contemplation, undertaken for its own sake rather than as a means to an end. Perfection is enjoyed without ulterior motive, simply because it is a superior way of being. The element of achievement consists of being able to stay in its presence. Whereas rites of passage aim at achieving membership of a particular level of human society, one which usually signifies a more mature relationship with a god, the purpose of religion which contemplates divine perfection is to abandon consciousness of the world as long, and as often, as possible. Rites of passage play a restricted role, concerned with entry into and final departure from the ordinary world. The place where we are going is one which we would never choose to leave. It is the place of perfection.

There are elements of this kind of spirituality in all religions. It would be hard to imagine one which had no construct of perfection, or one in which the construct was less than salient. If salient, then available; whether or not the notion of a spiritual journey provides a root metaphor of religious thought, the sheer importance of perfection makes it a present reality (see Appendix I). It is not that we are perfect, but that we are aware of perfection as a spiritual fact, something to be dwelt on, and so, metaphorically speaking, dwelt in. Religions which divinise nature, human or otherwise, regard the journey enshrined in the rite in terms of real events taking place in the world. For these religions the voyage is itself part of the arrival, the whole event, voyage and arrival, constituting human religion, the experience of god in 'lived life' (to use Buber's term) (1961: 30). Though contemplation of divine perfection requires a kind of psycho-spiritual journey in order to attain the state of mind in which it can take place, the state of contemplation alone is of real value, infinitely more important than the spiritual exercises undertaken in order to achieve it. In other words, the real value lies 'outside' the world rather than 'inside' it.

All the same, the vision of perfection acts upon conscious awareness at various levels, providing us with a source of *immediate* refreshment, one which is not restricted by membership of a particular religion, with its repertoire of rites and schools of meditation and contemplation. God's perfection refreshes mind and spirit in works of art which are intentionally religious, and in the perfection of those which are not. Popular forms of religious expression, enjoyed by those who do not regard themselves as particularly 'religious' and do not belong to a definite religious tradition, mediate the vision of a transcendent wholeness to vast numbers of people. The imagery of perfection functions at a deeper level than this, however. According to Jung it is the most important component of mankind's unconscious mind (1959, 1976, 1977, 1983). Dramatherapy provides us with powerful evidence of the truth of this.

'The square in the circle, the circle in the square.' Time and again, in the imagery of dramatherapy, the mandala makes itself present, reconciling and blessing. The 'primordial image of psychic totality' presents original wholeness, balance and perfection – creation known as a divine work of art, the experience of God's own identity and intention. It is an image that occurs frequently throughout the religions of the world (McGuire and Hull, 1978: 327, 328). Whatever the specific doctrine may be, the message is always one of healing through the resolution of disharmony: in other words, the restoration of wholeness. A vision of perfection unites conflicting elements within the divine harmony – the balance and perfection of the divine intention, which is fundamental to our nature as part of God's creation.

As we saw in the last section, human creativity tends always towards the achievement of productive syntheses, ideas which solve one set of problems while suggesting another. Our notions of what is perfect must take account of the creation of still more perfection, a more satisfactory balance, new kinds of completeness. To this extent the ideas of the gestalt psychologists were incomplete: the closure we seek always contains an openness, which is the anticipation of future fulfilment, the imaging forth of pregnant conclusions. Although we are not aware of it, our personal construct systems are continually modifying themselves in order to enable us to predict an unknown future, so that the confidence we feel is the result of openness, not finality. Patterns evolve spirally, seeking stability at every stage. This is reflected in myths and legends about creativity and creation:

A prince refuses to marry and provide heirs for his father. He publicly announces his intention to turn his back on the world, and his father imprisons him. Meanwhile, far away in a distant land, a princess is imprisoned for similar reasons. The Jinnayeh of an ancient well takes the sleeping prince under his special protection. Another Jinnayeh tells the first one about the sleeping princess of whom *he* has become protector on the other side of the world.

The Jinnayehs argue as to which is more beautiful, prince or princess? The second Jinnayeh transports the princess to the prince's bed to compare the two. They are still not able to agree which is more beautiful. In desperation, the first Jinnayeh calls an Ifrit, who suggests that the sleepers should be awakened, to see which would be the more amazed by the other's beauty. First the prince is awakened, and falls in love at first sight, before being sent back to sleep. The princess, when she wakes, sees her own ring on the prince's finger and is overcome with even greater love and admiration. Having lost the contest, she is transported back home. With her ring as talisman, the prince sets out to find her, and to be re-united with the other half of himself...

This Arabian tale retains the shape of a creation myth, reproducing the similarity and novelty which constitutes true creativity. The story itself may be used in a dramatherapy session, in its original form or adapted in some way or other to suit the occasion. The way in which characters and events balance gives the action a comforting simplicity, while the story itself is vivid and exciting. It would be easy enough to see how a dramatherapy group would set about constructing a similar tale. Novelty unfolds as characters or happenings are called into being, while the shape of the tale gives people a clue about what form their imagination ought to take.

   The story is paradigmatic of the creative gesture in its narrative form. We have already looked at dramatherapy as a privileged time and place in which we search for truth and are healed in the searching. Now we consider it as the enterprise of recreating the world and ourselves as part of the world. The imagery of dramatherapy moulds itself upon the mandala, which in itself mediates the presence of order and the underlying truths of divine perfection. We have seen that the dramatherapeutic setting reproduces what Northrop Frye calls 'the point of epiphany' whose 'most common settings are the mountain top, the island, the tower, the lighthouse, and the ladder or staircase' (1957: 302). All of these are noted for being set apart or lifted up: places of encounter or enlightenment. The mandala on the other hand is the presence of original perfection as that which does not have to be attained, but simply enjoyed.

Dramatherapy makes contact with the desire to construct, to give order to an unruly universe by making something of it. It is a co-operative making, in a setting which has been experienced as meaningful and life-like. What is made here will work because it has been well made, in a good heart, and validated by the free gift of a loving acceptance. There may be little technical skill, little time in which to arrive at a perfect expression or a feeling of an idea. This wish is well-made because it is spontaneous rather than because it has been practised. Personal meaning and human truth arise from the situation in the rapid flowering which occurs when men and women lose their fear of contact and reach out to one another to understand and be understood, accept and be accepted. This is religion as creation: the spiritual experience of possibility which emerges from the sharing of human spiritual aspiration, which Durkheim claimed to be the prototype of religion. So far as that goes, the evidence is against him; there are other valid religious phenomena than those associated with 'représentations collectives' (Lukes, 1975: 6–8). That it is a valid form of religious experience is beyond dispute, however. It, too, is experienced in dramatherapy.

Out of the desire to share comes the awareness that a new spiritual reality is emerging. This is difficult to describe, although a kind of dream-like merging of identity is involved. It is the 'peace that passeth understanding', pre-conceptual in origin. The group itself is felt to be united in a new corporate personality which is more real, more potent, but much less distinct than each individual within it. This is difficult to express in psychological terms, and even harder to account for. One way would be to say that it is the surrender of defensiveness that produces a holistic effect. So long as we are determined to 'keep ourselves to ourselves' and refuse to 'give' at all in our attitude to the rest of the group, nothing new will happen. The group will not come to life. If, however, we can find a way of relaxing our defences, the group will assume an identity which we recognise as being its own, a 'somebody' who is not merely the sum of the various people who comprise it, but a new factor, 'we' as well as 'I'. What we have, in fact, is a number of 'I's plus a 'we' – a true holism. As Sue Jennings often says, the group is 'consciously individual at the same time as being consciously social'.

It is this new factor, the consciousness of corporate identity, which is always present when the group meets, and must be taken into account by each member as a kind of unconditioned variable, a joker in the pack. It allows the group to express its natural creativity. This is the creativity of each of its members set free by a situation in which the circumstances of personal identity are changed by group membership, and all sorts of things could happen. Or so it seems. Kelly describes how personal construct systems, the way people organise their expectations of the world, become looser, more permeable, by ideas which are not already tried and tested parts of our mental stock-in-trade. By letting go of established patterns of thought we are able to see things in new ways (1955: 528). Unless we loosen our cognitive grasp on the world, our mental picture will never change. Unless we tighten it again, we have no efficient way of using the new constructs we have included in our system, and the new shape it has achieved. It is the same kind of interchange as the one that Buber and Williams describe. (See Chapter 2.)

Creativity and spirituality are linked in so far as both are experiences of psychological novelty, coming into the human situation 'from the outside'. They are experiences of attainment rather than struggle, arrival rather than progression, perfection rather than aspiration. Their metaphor is not a road but a rose – perhaps the one commented on by Gertrude Stein! Many people regard creative experience as their own kind of spirituality (which is not quite the same as calling great artists of the past 'immortal'), and religious artists have great difficulty in distinguishing the two, the second translating itself spontaneously into the language of the first. In dramatherapy terms, this is artistry at its simplest and most direct, as groups conjure beauty out of the air simply by being together and enjoying the fact of sharing. It can be expressed in noisiness or silence, standing or sitting, movement or repose. To begin with, people need to find ways of 'discovering' the rose. Sessions usually begin with activities designed to help people let loose their shyness, to forget themselves and find interest in whatever is going on, and who is involved in it. Only then will they enjoy being together in the group, standing in a ring and holding hands; feeling the strength and confidence of sharing responsibility for whatever happens next.

This kind of process usually occurs at the beginning of a session, and sometimes, too, at the end. It may be quiet, a time of simply enjoying being together again, making someone feel welcome, finding out how people have been since the group last met, assessing how they are now. It may be a noisy game in which people are encouraged to make as much row as possible and really let themselves go. It should be a group game rather than one involving teams, as the element of competition is to be avoided at this introductory stage of the process. One of the best ways of using the group potential is to perform a 'circle dance', in which everybody stands round, holds hands, and dances together. This is a continuous dance, in which everyone follows the same steps each in her or his way. This goes on for some minutes, stirring up the creative spirit, spinning people into the main process of the session.

This introductory phase uses set forms to produce a state of mutual trust and corporate enjoyment which is able to take imaginative flight in whatever emerges. Creativity proves to be as contagious as any other human state of mind; more contagious in fact, because of its essential openness, its identity as that which reaches outward from itself to set another person's imagination aflame, and so carry the torch onwards. Just as God creates life, so human beings image forth new ideas and experiences, new ways of seeing and understanding. Just as God's creativity is an expression of his love, which in turn creates love, so human creativity emerges from relationship and gives rise to new kinds of relationship. To create a work of art or be present at the birth of a shared imaginative experience is to do something which possesses a primal rightness. To create something is, after all, the oldest activity of all, as well as being the source of all newness. It is to make space for life. At the level of creativity the spiritual nature of dramatherapy is self-evident.

The Session

The following is an account of a dramatherapy workshop which took place at the National Conference of the British Association for Dramatherapists, held at Newcastle Polytechnic in September 1990. There were 15 people involved, slightly more women than men. The process took place in a large square room with a low roof and very few windows. This is mentioned because it seemed to contribute to a rather concentrated atmosphere, despite the feeling of space within the room. Music was playing from a record player at one side of the room as people wandered in. The teacher wandered among them, encouraging them to look more closely at the room. What sort of room was it? What did it remind them of? Perhaps it held memories they'd like to share? Things they'd rather keep to themselves? They should try to concentrate without speaking, and could sit, stand, crawl, lie flat – anything they wanted, *if* they wanted. They could close their eyes if they wanted, or keep them open to watch people and see what they were doing. They could examine textures and resonances. They could do nothing at all – simply let things go on around them. Whatever they did, they must do it without speaking. The leader spoke calmly and clearly. When he had finished he kept quiet for several minutes.

He spoke again. There was a shade more excitement in his voice. Perhaps they would like to approach someone and look at them. They had never seen another person, but they could see that whatever it was, it was like *them*. They could explore a little, treating it with respect as something like themselves. They should find out without offending. When they had finished they should sit down facing each other and just look at each other. After a minute the leader announced that they had 'reached the first horizon'. What should they call it? How would they describe what they had been doing? Straight-away somebody said 'exploration', and the leader wrote this on the black-board in capital letters.

He said, 'Now we've explored a bit, we'll go on to look a bit deeper.' He suggested that people should begin to speak to the person they had just discovered, sharing things about themselves – their name, their work, the kind of things they liked or didn't like, something funny that they think would make the other person laugh etc., etc. – he would leave it to them, after all it was their relationship. The conversations began quietly, and gradually grew in intensity. The leader wandered among the couples, not staying more than a few minutes in any place, and not saying anything. He moved over to the record player and turned the volume up slightly. It was a particularly well-loved piece, the Adagietto from Mahler's Fifth Symphony, and some of the people in the room began to pay attention to it. Someone said, 'Oh listen – I love this.' The leader said, 'We'll lie back and listen to the music for a bit – have a break from talking. Let your body relax. What was that your partner said that gave you a clue about them, the kind of person they are? Think about it for a moment as you listen to the music.' After a pause he began to speak again, more gently, with intervals between the words: 'Consider life... and death... what do you see? Consider truth... and God... can you see a picture, a person, a place? If you can't don't worry, you mustn't force this. Another time, perhaps, another place... Don't worry. If you can, however [*he turned the music off sharply*], I want you to cling on to what you see. No, don't tell me, tell your partner. Share with your partner. If you've nothing to share, share that. First, though, will someone who has something to report come and write something on the board. Put "discovery" under "exploration".'

The leader went round the room negotiating with individuals and partnerships so that people who had nothing perceptible to report would be included in groups containing someone who had. This resulted in the formation of three groups. When the man or woman who had arrived at some kind of image told his or her group what this consisted of, there were exclamations of recognition from other members, including several people who had not been conscious of any definite image. A member of each group lit a candle and the group stood in a circle around it. The purpose of this, the leader explained, was to celebrate the revelation to one or more of the group members of a way of perceiving truth that was usually hidden or distorted in conscious awareness, and to give honour to it. The leader suggested that the groups might like to create a rite for their own 'picture'.

What would be the central 'happening' in such a rite? He wrote 'celebration' on the blackboard and the groups began to experiment. One group, centred upon the image of a flower, portrayed the opening of a rose; another communicated 'the road through life' in a series of episodes; the last formed itself into a mountain. This was all carried out with a minimum of solemnity but a good deal of concentration. Each group showed its work to the others. The leader asked if the people who had not experienced any ideas or thought-pictures during the music had been able to enjoy being part of the rites. All except one said that they had. The workshop ended with members forming into two lines, each person holding hands with his or her partner and moving, dragon-fashion, around the room.

This workshop is based upon the experiences of loosening and tightening, the 'creativity cycle' described by Kelly. The process of loosening of habitual reactions and associations begins as soon as those taking part start to become aware of their environment in new ways, and increases as people are given permission to welcome each other into a relaxed and trusting relationship and to let their minds follow the patterns created by the music. The tightening phase begins when those taking part concentrate their awareness upon a particular image and develop this until it can be presented as something to be shared with other people, a symbol of encounter.

An Example of a Creation Myth (Hindu)

The First Movement

The Turtle Man has married 13 daughters of the Lord of Virtue who is even older than he. Two of the daughters have given birth, one to the Titans, the other to the Gods. These two races are perpetually at war. The Titan high priest persuades Shiva to give him a charm to revive the Titan dead, so as to gain the advantage over the Gods. The Gods, therefore, consult Brahma and Vishnu, who advise them to make a truce with their enemies, which will allow them to obtain the 'nectar of deathlessness' by churning the Ocean of Immortal Life. This ushers in the second movement.

The Second Movement

The Gods use Mt Mandora as churning-stick, and Vasuki, King of Serpents as rope; Vishnu, in the form of a tortoise supports the base of the churning-stick; the Gods hold one end of Vasuki, the Titans the other. They churn away for a thousand years, bringing forth Kaluka, the concentrated power of death. Shiva swallows him. Next, other forms of concentrated power emerge — nymphs (Apsarases), Lakshmi (the goddess of fortune). Uchchaihshravas (a milk-white horse), Kaustubha (the pearl of gems), plus five other precious sources of power, ending with Dhanvantari, the physician of the Gods, who holds Amrita, the moon, the cup of life, in his hand.

The Final Movement

Gods and Titans struggle for the cup. Rahu, a Titan, manages to steal a sip, but is beheaded. (His head is forever chasing after the moon!) Because the Titans seem to be winning, Vishnu takes the form of a beautiful dancer in order to distract them, and passes the cup to the Gods. He then transforms himself into a mighty warrior and helps the Gods drive the Titans into the canyons and crags of the underworld. And so the Gods dine forever on Amrita atop Mt Sumera, the world's central mountain.

The story possesses all the excitement of the Hero's Quest, with the symmetry of a typical creation myth. Gods and Titans are equally opposed and each has to seek help from elsewhere in order to have a chance of winning. The charm given by Shiva in the first movement corresponds to the cup Amrita which is the object of attention in the final movement. Most important of all, however, is the status of the second movement, the actual movement of creation. This plays a wholly positive part in the myth's structure, expressing creation rather than change or progression. The Ocean of Immortal Life is churned to produce the chaos of formlessness from which persons and objects will emerge; but the action is purposeful and the involvement of the Gods intentional. This is no hiatus in ordinary reality when the machinery of the normal world is thrown out of gear by an influx of holiness. Here the entire scenario, all three movements plus their *dramatis personae*, is holy, and the heart of the story describes them at their most effective.

It is astonishing to see how these significant patterns, which refer to an underlying (or overarching) religious consciousness reveal themselves in dramatherapy. For instance, a group of four women and four men all complained of inhibiting sexual problems. After being encouraged to intro- duce themselves to one another, they were told that they could arrange themselves anywhere in the space provided, on one side or the other of a row of chairs placed down the middle of the room. A blank space had been left half way down the row, making a kind of gateway from one side to the other. Everybody walked round for a few minutes, passing backwards and forwards through the gap. Soon, however, the men gravitated to one side of the division, and the women to the other. The women were given the subject of 'fashion' to discuss, the men that of 'football'. Each group could include all or some members of the other in its discussion. Generally speaking, once they had been polarised in this way, both groups were uncomfortable. Given permission to invite members in from the other side, they stayed where they were; but one of the men moved up to the gap and humorously asked for volunteers. After a few seconds he was joined by one of the women. They stayed in the gap, effectively closing it by drawing chairs across.

The wall was still there, with its gap, at the beginning of the second session. The two who had been sitting in the gap immediately went over and started moving all the chairs, dismantling the wall. The others helped them to do this. People seemed to be undecided as to where to put the chairs, but it was eventually agreed that they should be placed along the walls: 'To give us lots of room.' Somebody remarked on the fact that the room now looked rather empty, and the man who had been the first to break ranks and address the women said 'We'll put a chair in the middle, then'. He grabbed hold of a chair and placed it in the centre of the room, pretending to stumble and drop it. One of the women asked who the chair was for?

After discussion, it was finally decided that its purpose was to provide a focal point: 'We can sit round it instead of each side of a wall.' The dramatherapist pointed out that they did not need to sit and talk. 'You've got plenty of room – enjoy it. You can use the chairs if you want.' The group decided they would do this, in order to make a wall round the space rather than to divide it up. As before they left an entrance. Now the resemblance to a garden was clear. Seeing some of them looking askance, not knowing what to do with this new inviting space, the therapist reminded them that it was perfectly all right to use the imagination. She suggested that each choose a partner of the opposite sex and plan out a quadrant of the garden working inwards from the wall to the central chair, or outwards from chair to wall. This took quite a long time, as the couples needed to discuss, and sometimes argue, about how to do things. When they had finished, they described their segment of the circular garden to the others, inviting them in to have a closer look at the flowers and shrubs. 'Don't just look, touch them. Get to know how they feel. Smell them, breathe them into yourself. Tell me what the soil feels like. Share it all with your partner. I want you to find a place on a garden path to lie down and relax. Let your mind relax and see what comes into it. What can you see?' Most people saw things connected with flowers and gardens. Somebody said 'It's a rose', and several people, men and women, echoed this.

'The garden is a rose. The part we're in is the heart of the rose, and its petals fall outward over the wall. Over the world. What colour is it? What does it feel like? Take your time, then find your partner and talk about it.' The session drew to an end with the men and women holding hands in a circle round the central chair and talking gently about the garden and the rose: 'We went into the garden and came out as the rose.' The process was therapeutic in that the imagery of invasion and engulfment gave way before that of inclusion and expansion; terror at the prospect of losing individual integrity metamorphosed into an experience of personal wholeness which came from living 'inside the mandala'.

Postscript

In this book I have tried to look at dramatherapy from the point of view of what I consider to be its innate spirituality. The spirituality of dramatherapy is subliminal because it is never stated in religious terms, or even by analogy with theological doctrines, but refers to an underlying image or metaphor which gives shape to aspiration and meaning to history. In dramatherapy, the framework provides the setting for a potentially endless succession of images, by consciously reproducing the symbolism of the empty space, the 'centre of the world', in which everything originates and to which everything finally comes. Here the fundamentally religious nature of what is presented is entirely explicit, but usually non-verbal. Because of the kind of imagery employed, a sense of the sacredness of the enterprise is almost inescapable. There is no explicit reference to religion, however. There is no need; the process achieves a clarity beyond the scope of words.

At the same time, the approach is indirect. Both written story and acted drama seek to engage the emotions by means of arousing the imagination – a more effective way of delivering a message than simply spelling it out, because it involves a certain investment of self. We become identified with the characters in the book or the play, and regard what is happening to them as relevant to ourselves. This happens because meaning is not immediately obvious. In a book it hides behind a story that concerns somebody else, somebody with whom we may or may not be able to identify. In the kind of drama involved in dramatherapy, not only is the story different but the character may be bizarre and exotic, belonging to a totally different order of being. We may find ourselves in a world of heroes and heroines, demons and monsters, gods and goddesses.

Dramatherapy presents us with two ways of being less than explicit; by hiding a message behind a story about somebody else; by choosing some-body as a protagonist or character whose identity is already itself masked –

a personage of religious mythology in whom humanity symbolises divinity, or somebody human within a drama that is not simply different from ours but acted out on another plane of reality. Because in drama 'the medium is the message', barriers like these are gateways opening upon the experience of identification, contributing to the process of 'building up consciously contrived aesthetic distance in order to secure a richer personal involvement – an involvement which is authentically imaginative *because it cannot be anything else*' (Grainger, 1990: 20). The stranger the world of the drama, the more eager we are to lose ourselves in it. The reason for this is simple enough. It is when I am immediately confronted by a situation like my own and a person like myself that I retreat behind the barrier of my own psychological defence mechanisms; it is when the message is clear, and clearly addressed to me, that I try to evade it. The refusal of drama to be explicit, its determination to appear to be talking about someone and something else, lead me to relax my vigilance, and I feel I am in a safe place with friends. And then, once I have relaxed, the action takes hold of me and I am seized by the implicit.

The characteristics of dramatherapy that have been chosen because they resemble religion are not unique to 'artistic' therapy. Although this is true, it is unlikely that other examples could be found within psychotherapy which would be more strikingly religious in implication or statement. Dramatherapy stands out, however, as a way of embodying the yearnings of the human spirit, within a setting specifically designed for their therapeutic expression. Within this setting, in terms of these images, the secular cannot avoid having spiritual implications. An examination of the other 'artistic therapies' undertaken from this point of view would yield similar results, although it should not be assumed that they would be exactly the same. Dramatherapy clings to a directness of expression which in some other therapies may be clouded by interpretation. The processes of dramatherapy do not reveal something, they *are* something. If psychoanalytic 'explanation' has been already provided, the significance of those metaphors is obscured, if not actually discounted. Wherever there is artistic expression, however, there is the possibility of direct, unclouded revelation.

Whether or not dramatherapy can be said to correspond to what Yinger has called 'secular patterns infused with a religious quality' (1970: 191) is open to question. I have argued that the imagery of dramatherapy is spiritual at a level *preceding* explicit statement. In other words, it is *very* spiritual. In fact, dramatherapy is not the 'pattern infused with religious quality', so much as the religious quality that infuses the pattern. In one case, the pattern is the institution of the National Health Service which is gradually employing more and more therapists who communicate professionally in this way without drawing attention to the fact − or even, in some cases, even knowing that they do so. In this case, the 'secular alternative to religion' is a branch of the health service which functions within the territory traditionally occupied by the various forms of spiritual healing. Metaphor mediates insight that can be accepted or rejected, or simply lived with. By translating life into pictures and stories, the possibility of a wider picture, a more profound story presents itself. Within a setting of reductionist philosophies and instrumental techniques such an approach speaks for itself (see Appendix II).

Equally revealing is the way, and also the speed, with which dramatherapy has spread. People who are suffering from an identifiable psychiatric illness; those passing through a period of painful adjustment or who have suffered recent trauma; those who find relationships difficult or are afraid of 'doing things in public'; those who have simply discovered the spiritual refreshment that dramatherapy affords; all these, and many more, are turning in this direction for help. Could it be that for a steadily growing number of people it fulfils at least part of the role traditionally played by religion?

Perhaps it is still a little early to say. However, I am sure that the suggestion could not have been made at all 20 years ago. Who knows what the situation may be when the artistic therapies have finally left the shelter of the institutions that have protected them up to now and have launched out into the world? More and more groups are running workshops on an independent basis throughout Britain. Up to now they have been largely ignored by churches, although not necessarily by church people. It will be interesting to see how long it will be before 'official' religion begins to take notice − and how it will react when it does. Will it prove flexible enough to acknowledge the value of a non-ecclesiastical, mainly non-propositional, ally in the search for truth?

In a sense, however, the support and involvement of organised religion is not the point. Dramatherapy is significant in and for itself as a spiritual activity taking place in a secular setting. On one hand it benefits from the experience of certain religious movements of the mid-twentieth century (e.g. the dominant faith-ethos of the 1960s, with its emphasis on intuition, candour and expressiveness, later allied to charismatic spontaneity and willingness to be adventurous); on the other, it represents a movement on the part of medicine itself to become more spiritual, more willing to countenance a more poetic interpretation of wholeness. In the second half of the twentieth century, religion plays a different role in society from those it has played before. It is neither a 'social cement' binding individuals together to prevent conflict, nor a 'social opium' sedating antagonistic groups and classes. In its former institutionalised form it no longer looks after society's 'soul' in exchange for a share of the community wealth. In a highly organised yet socially isolating capitalist state, religion is a minority interest, making its own arrangements with individuals. The huge congregations of the charismatic and fundamentalist churches are islands in the sea of those who 'have their own faith'.

At one level, then, dramatherapy provides one of many alternative opportunities for the intensely individual, relationship-centred spirituality of today to express itself, without having to tie itself down to any actual religious beliefs (see Appendix II). This kind of thing is by no means new of course. Writing in the last century, Georg Simmel described a time when religious activity,

> which formerly manifested itself through the development of more adequate dogmatic contents, could no longer express itself through the polarity of a believing subject and a believing object. In the ultimate state of affairs towards which this new tendency is coming, religion would function as a medium for the direct expression of life. (1968: 23)

To a large extent Simmel's prophecy has come true. Citizens of twentieth-century industrialised democracy express their spiritual awareness in the way they interpret their experiences rather than by means of direct statement (Bailey, 1989). Their means of social and personal self-expression may be chosen because of the opportunity for 'religion in solution'; their religious awareness is expressed within their general experience. All the same it requires satisfaction even in its diffused state. Because religion and health are perceived as implying each other, spiritual values may be expressed and spiritual satisfactions enjoyed within a therapeutic setting. Here, people may consider themselves to be in touch with underlying truths in ways that are personal and yet social, without having to be personally involved with what is felt to be an impersonal, even repressive, institution. The therapeutic group provides both transcendence and well-being, in the form of an available otherness that is the source of both inspiration and comfort. It may not be religion at its most intense and intellectual; it would not satisfy St John of the Cross – but it is a kind of baring of the soul, a kind of reaching out to the source of meaning and as such it is essentially religious.

This kind of diffused belonging is more in line with traditional religion than might at first be supposed. Its association with health agencies gives it the prestige of belonging to a genuinely social institution, one which represents the preoccupations of society, in ways that religion does not.

Sociologically speaking, any blurring of the borders between religion and medicine has the effect of rescuing 'official' religion from its isolated and fragmented condition and helps it to rediscover its social identity as a source of spiritual inspiration and personal well-being. The position of dramatherapy within the NHS presents health care as a vehicle of religious awareness, an opportunity for its expression within a situation in which official, explicit, religious structures have lost their appeal because they were never intended to provide a society educated for and nurtured in individualism with the kind of private – even secret – religion it naturally prefers (Turner, 1991: 107). Even if the content of dramatherapy, its subject matter of myth, symbol and story did not imply religion, its social function within the NHS as an opportunity for individual expression and personal self-discovery within a group setting would certainly do so.

Finally, as 'official' religion becomes de-institutionalised, more spontaneous in its expression and less rigid in its social identity, so healing strives to overcome the restricted definitions it has imposed upon itself, and opportunities occur for the healing power of faith and the spiritual dimensions of healing to meet and recognise themselves in one another. Although dramatherapy has gained credibility as a therapeutic modality by its association with the state health service, it is by no means limited to this by working within the framework of 'institutionalised medicine'. Most dramatherapists work independently of either public or private medicine. This means in effect that there are two kinds of dramatherapeutic practice: one which is 'medical' and one which is not. 'Medical' dramatherapy is only so by association, certainly; but this particular alignment makes it part of an extremely exclusive company of allied professions, namely the health team of a local health authority. Freelance dramatherapists will have received identical training and work in the same way; they will belong to the same professional organisation and attend the same annual conference; at the same time, they work independently, outside any organised health provision.

There is a good deal of evidence suggesting that the spiritual awareness implicit in dramatherapy has emerged in a whole range of applications and expressions, and is continuing to do so. A question that might be asked is, how far are these developments willing to go in acknowledging their origins in orthodox dramatherapy? How formal (i.e. self-conscious) is their resemblance to the original? There is room here for further investigation.

In the arts therapies the dialogue between science and faith, intuition and intellect, seems to have gone underground. It works away to bring unity to our fragmented longing for wholeness. Healing is indivisible, longing everywhere to overcome the institutional and philosophical divisions that seek to limit and control its scope so that it can express the wholeness that is its nature and its name. As Durkheim argued, the reality which is crucial to our lives as human beings is not the physical milieu but our interpretation of it, the systems of norms and rules which makes social behaviour possible. In order to make sense of our striving for spirituality we must reverse the perspective which sees society as the result of individual behaviour and see it as its cause: consciously or unconsciously, individuals act in the light of a socially prescribed view of the universe which they have assimilated. At the heart of such a view, and working as its organising principle, are certain great oppositions, paradigms of definition and significant division. These may or may not be perceived in religious terms as sacred and profane, heaven and hell, God and the devil; they are certainly understood morally, in terms of contrasting values – good and evil, selfish and altruistic, lightness and dark, ice and fire, etc. One of the most important of them is the opposition between sickness and health which lies right at the heart of human meaning, intertwined with those other great constructs in the code which we use to make sense of life, the social system which establishes us in our private identity by giving us a language in which to talk about our deepest and most personal concerns. At this highest level of our personal meaning system we find ourselves sharing a network of ideas and feelings about what we interpret as 'life itself' – life contrasted with death. Both life and death are part of the meaning that sustains our world and with which we sustain ourselves, the language that we use to describe our world (Schechner, 1988: 247). At the highest level of our spiritual awareness the ideas combine, participating in a super-ordinate notion of wholeness, an ultimate metaphysical perfection which is the final meaning of all persons everywhere, the ultimate truth of human life. To have this kind of awareness – the awareness that can only be transmitted as living metaphor – is to receive a kind of healing that defies the restrictions imposed by definition.

I believe that such healing is in dramatherapy's gift. It is all too easy to underestimate drama, to consider it as recreation and nothing more – a way of letting off steam in public without having to suffer unpleasant social consequences, of enjoying vicarious satisfaction at the expense of reality, or simply an adult version of 'let's pretend'. Because we are allowed to become involved with the stage happening without leaving our seats, we are able to titillate ourselves with the experience of imaginary escapes and deliverances, and so achieve the perverse satisfaction we associate with pressing a tooth that is only painful when touched – a kind of Aunt Sally cleverly set up for us to throw our personal reality at. There is of course a measure of truth in all this: as Schechner puts it 'these performances are liminal events existing to mediate or explore for pleasure interactions that are potentially risky and disruptive'. He points to rites of passage as a clear example: 'Where trouble is liable to break out, theatrical fun eases the way' (1988: 247).

This is too easy, however. We have seen that drama works at a deeper level than this. The central movement of the rite of passage is not simply self- (and other-) indulgent fun; but the reality of actual changes. Only if the former situation is felt to have been really destroyed – if we ourselves have been personally involved in dismantling it in order to build the future anew – can we experience real change. At the heart of drama there lies, not the indulgence of fantasy, but the gift of symbol. The two things are very different. Fantasy is essentially private, created by the self out of itself for the purposes of its own delight. Symbol reaches away from the self, taking others with it. The images of fantasy delight and frustrate themselves rather than what they point to. In reaching for the unknown we seek what is outside ourselves and are deepened and expanded both by the action itself and the relationship that it permits. Rites of passage function because they create a powerful symbol of personal transformation. For those taking part they constitute the avoidance of fantasy solutions and the painful creation of a real future. This cannot be imagined, but only discovered. Step by step the novice penetrates the barrier of the unknown as actor and spectator make their way through the play in search of revelation of a wider truth, a more personal relationship to life. Disbelief is suspended as an action of will, so that a new kind of belief may be established.

This is what happens in the most solemn exorcism and the most hilarious farce. Wherever meaning is shared as it is in dramas and corporate rituals of all kinds, however theatrically presented, private fantasy is transformed into public reality. Drama is revealed as a 'transitional object' – the mere action of staging renders an action symbolic of a wider truth, wider and more inclusive than our efforts to contain it as part of our immediate experience, part of ourselves. By means of drama and theatre, fantasy becomes symbol, alive with the promise that is also a presence, leading us across into a more personal future. The presence that is alive and active in drama is nothing less than the spiritual truth of relationship, which is the truth of being human. Drama discloses drama; we take part in the demonstration of who and what we are.

We are the ones who constructed the drama, the play, the ritual. In it we put more than we know how to; into it we build a symbolism that we feel to be greater than ourselves, to originate elsewhere. Our own understanding and experience provides us with a metaphor whose richness can never be exhausted, a personal poetry that touches each individual in a different way;

in friendship and love, grief and joy, we make contact with one antoher in metaphors of profound spiritual resonance, which colour our experience of the society in which we live. Just as our dramas and rituals reflect and affect society, so society affects and reflects the kind of plays and rituals we perform. Our dramatic experience of life and of plays about life revolves around metaphors of ultimate human meaning, which are always images of an achievable perfection of personal relationship. 'Human beings' says Victor Turner, 'learn through experience, though all too often they repress painful experience.' He goes on: 'Perhaps the deepest experience is through drama; not through social drama or stage drama (or its equivalent) alone but in the circulatory or oscillatory process of their mutual and incessant modification' (1985: 301). Society and art continually meet and draw apart again as their relationship is one of reinforcement and criticism, union and separation, safety and danger. The drama itself centres upon the movement from Thou to It; whatever metaphor is presented in play or rite, both are symbols of the truth of human encounter, the life of betweenness, which is theirs simply because they are drama. As drama, they touch without grasping, caress without wounding, discover without colonising, perpetually leaving room for what is but cannot be told. This is drama's central metaphor and the spiritual heart of dramatherapy.

Appendices

Appendices

APPENDIX I

Root Metaphors

Some stories have a greater resonance than others. This obviously applies to religious narratives because their subject matter makes greater claim to explicit significance than non-religious subjects do. Their subjects claim to possess divine authority. Similarly, stories involving the archetypes of the collective unconscious 'speak to our condition' in a way that ordinary narratives cannot. It has often been pointed out that for an 'ordinary' story to be at all memorable it must have at least the suggestion of an archetype somewhere! The metaphors we have examined are each of them expressed at some point in terms of archetypal imagery.

These stories are particularly valuable because of their ability to explain human reality. Other kinds of story are important because of their ability to throw light on the process of story-making itself. Our stories express an idea as to how meaning itself works. We have stories about stories. At root these hermeneutic stories are metaphors of certain kinds of action. In his 'root metaphor' theory, Stephen Pepper provides a useful tool for understanding the way we understand the world: 'The appearance of a great number of different world theories arises simply from the great numbers of combinations that can be made out of the parts of seven or eight complex objects' (1942: 329). He goes on to discuss four hypotheses which, he says, underly all the rest. These hypotheses take the form of metaphorical events.

The set – arranging things in order by similarity and dissimilarity (formism).

The machine – something working on something else to attain or produce something (mechanism).

The historic event – incidents in the drama of life that 'fall into place' in retrospect (contextualism).

The system – creating form and balance, in which elements imply one another (organicism).

The significance of the root metaphor lies in its ability to stand for an ultimate category of explanation. It does this by by-passing analysis and finding a convenient analogy in basic human experience, something able to throw light on the way life 'works' (mechanist), or 'works out' (contextualist); the way things 'develop' (organicist) or 'fit in' (formist). No-one claims that root metaphors are testable in a scientific sense. In fact, two of them forestall scientific thought; the underlying impulse towards scientific method is based on argument drawn from the formist and mechanist metaphors. They have a wider application than individual symbols, whatever may be the archetypal resonance of a particular symbol. The application of a root metaphor is intended to be universal. Some are more successful at this than others are, but each metaphor is particularly good at presenting a fundamental way of looking at life itself.

Their specifically spiritual identity lies in their ability to present us with a primitive sign picture of the way reality can be seen to make sense as a whole – in other words, an ur-metaphor. Any one of these hypotheses satisfies the first of Geertz's (1968) 'three points where chaos threatens to break in on man', the problem of making sense of *how* things happen. What they cannot do is to satisfy our natural need to know *why* they should happen – and why they should involve us in so much pain and conflict. In order to gain knowledge about these things, which are also the substance of religious experience, we need personal reassurance as well as intellectual explanation, and must look elsewhere.

Root metaphors do not possess the same religious significance as archetypes, which provide the link between individual personal experience and truth of a kind that can authenticate itself as ultimate and inclusive, and which, by enabling the individual self to live in hope with its unanswered questions go far towards providing answers for them. The root metaphor remains a hypothesis, a kind of 'visual aid' for intellect; the archetype impresses our awareness with a significance that is not ours, although it refers to us. All the same, root metaphors are relevant as a way of comparing systems of thought. People approach the task of making sense of the universe in different ways: 'We relate to symbols differently', says Elizabeth Rees, 'and forge our own language of imagery and our own response to life' (1992). How can it be otherwise when our spiritual journeys are so different?

> Each of us has embarked on a unique path to discover our roots and our destiny; on the Journey we find that our story is deeply interwoven with that of others, but it is a testimony to the inexhaustible variety of creation and the immense lavishness of God that no life-story ever duplicates another. The hero-journey of each of us is necessary to complete the unfolding story of the world.' (1992: 100)

In a sense the context of our stories is not in our hands; it consists of those relationships, events and ideas that possess intense personal significance; times when we are conscious of having come face to face with ourselves and with life; occasions of significance which have no obvious purpose or intention, when truth has been mediated by archetype; officially important land-marks; decisions and resolutions of an existential kind. The transformation of these things into recognisable personal stories requires a method of explaining things which is articulate, consistent and effective. This is where the root metaphor proves so useful, as something which gives its own kind of meaning to our stories.

Certainly the role of metaphor is crucial. Whereas religious thought usually prefers to homologise metaphysical awareness with natural experience, so that it may give ordinary life explicit religious significance by rendering it permanently or intrinsically metaphorical, the kind of therapeutic approach represented by dramatherapy employs metaphor in a more focused and direct way as a means of contacting overarching meanings. Metaphor is invoked rather than simply assumed. Dramatherapy sessions are an anteroom of spirit.

Because dramatherapy uses metaphor to reveal meaning, the characteristic of metaphor that is most treasured is that of balance and completeness, as this is expressed in ideas of clarity and focus. The root metaphor of dramatherapy is consequently organicism, the image in which each part depends upon and contributes to every other. Pepper points out that contextualism, the metaphor of encounter, and organicism, which expresses coinherence, are closely related, the second developing from the first as relationship leads to closer degrees of mutuality and belonging. The cumulative series of contexts making up the *hero's journey* illustrates this strikingly, as does the notion of betweenness that is fundamental to dramatherapy. The *rite of passage*, which distinguishes and aligns states of social and religious being according to the formist metaphor, has an almost mechanistic feel to it. Similarly what I have called *the sojourn in heaven*, is basically formist: we are conformed to the image of perfection. The imagery of dramatherapy remains only potentially religious. It points away from itself but is not specific as to what it is pointing at. In a sense, however, this makes it more, not less, spiritual. It certainly reveals the capacity for spirit in the way we regard a whole range of secular structures. Metaphor tends always to the spiritual. At the fundamental level of root metaphor, all kinds of phenomena, individual, social, secular, religious, theological and therapeutic, are poeticised by their relationship to a wider truth.

An Investigation into Dramatherapists' Attitudes

Repertory Grids for Eleven Dramatherapists

1. Eleven dramatherapists, selected at random from the British Association for Dramatherapy membership list, constructed 'repertory grids' as a way of establishing the *degree* and *kind* of significance they attached to their own ways of evaluating the processes and techniques of dramatherapy.

2. A repertory grid is a way of getting people to reveal, in mathematical terms, the coherent view they have of a particular area of life, and how coherent that view is. It consists in a particular way of ordering the information about people and things that we are in the habit of using in order to understand them. In short 'elements' – that is the different parts of an overall mental picture – are related to one another in terms of constructs – the qualities or characteristics we choose to make sense of the relationships between and among them. George Kelly, who invented the approach, described a construct as 'a way in which two or more things are alike and *thereby* different from a third or more things' (1963). This 'way' is likely to be something we use whenever we think about these particular things, and others like them. In other words, it is part of our 'personal construct system' (1955, 1963).

3. The dramatherapists in this sample were asked to choose 12 elements from a list of 29 things associated with dramatherapy (Figure A.1). These consisted of techniques, interpersonal processes and kinds of subject matter familiar to all dramatherapists. They could be chosen at random, without bothering to put them in any order; the sole criterion was that all 12 should be things that the dramatherapist concerned had come into contact with at some point. The constructs were then elicited by the method mentioned by Kelly: that is, the first three elements were compared in order to discover what it was that distinguished two of them from the third. Whatever it was became the first construct. The method was repeated, using successive triads of elements (1 2 3, 2 3 4, 3 4 5, etc.) until there were (in this case) ten constructs (Figure A.2). These were made into a grid with the constructs along the top and the same number of elements down the left-hand side (Figure A.3).

Role-play

Role-play with animals

Role-reversal

Group 'warm-ups' (exercises)

Group 'contract'

Hero/heroine's journey

Fantasy journey (non-mobile)

Empty chair

Group game with individual responses

Group team game

Egoing (speaking as if you were the
    other person)

Mirroring

Sculpting (individual)

Sculpting (pairs)

Sculpting (group)

Masks

Magic shop

Puppets

Expressive dance

Story (acted with words)

Story (mimed)

Pantomime (knock about)

Myth

Fairy tale and legend

Mimed situations

Spectogram (symbolic arrangement
    of objects in a small space)

Exaggerated movement (macrocosm)

People and objects used
    metaphorically

Use of physical space to
    symbolise various kinds of
    'distance'

Figure A.1 Ad hoc list of elements associated with dramatherapy

4. The dramatherapists scored the elements in terms of the constructs, using
    a scale of 1–7 (1 = highest 'construct power' for a particular element, 7
    = the lowest, 4 = neither high nor low). For instance, a dramatherapist
    who had selected 'fantasy journey' from among the elements, and
    whose constructs contained 'symbolic', would probably put 1 at the
    point where they met. (See Figure A.3.)

5. The result is a grid which shows relationship scores and may be
    used to find out at a glance how strongly an individual associates a
    particular person, idea or thing with a particular way of assessing
    people, ideas and things. The relationship between elements and
    constructs is quite clear. Because of the grid arrangement, we are also
    able to gauge the amount of similarity between and among constructs;
    in other words we can see how closely an individual's ways of
    construing the world hang together, and gauge their ability to present
    an integrated view of things – in this case, of dramatherapy – and what
    kind of view that will be; in other words which constructs will be
    dominant within it.

1 Mirroring	1 Group	1 Fantasy
2 Animals (toy)	2 Imagination	2 Journey
3 Open-ended	3 Personalised	3 Epic
4 Fantasy	4 Interpretative	4 Group process
5 Surprise	5 Echoing	5 Standing outside self
6 Imagination	6 Metaphor	6 Embodiment
7 Unconscious symbolism	7 Use of medium	7 Wish-fulfilment
8 Identification	8 Direct approach	8 Magic
9 Empathy	9 Spontaneity	9 Story-line
10 Projective play	10 Creative	10 Selecting out detail

1 Role	1 Significant other	1 Personal insight
2 Reality orientation	2 Stimulus	2 Disarming focus
3 Interpersonal relationship	3 Metaphor	3 Personal responsibility
4 Imaginative space	4 Humour	4 Spontaneity
5 Narrative	5 Structure	5 Archetypes
6 Symbolic play	6 Action	6 Symbolic stories
7 Psychological distance	7 Relationship	7 Universality
8 Metaphor	8 Movement	8 Conflict of good and evil
9 Use of objects	9 Speaking from somewhere else	9 Body–mind intuition
10 Intrapersonal	10 Individual focus	10 Bodily Consciousness

1 Story	1 Pretending	1 Shape
2 Empathic use of language	2 Projective	2 Sympathy
3 Dramatic	3 Social vs individual	3 Imaginative
4 Direction-setting	4 Use of fantasy	4 Creative/outgoing
5 Reflecting	5 Child-like	5 Non-threatening
6 Relationship	6 Verbal	6 Slapstick
7 Use of role	7 Humour	7 Non-verbal
8 Exploratory	8 Theatrical	8 Narrative
9 Metaphor	9 Direct	9 Body
10 Group	10 Concerning internal mental life	10 Projective

1 Focus	1 Here
2 Intensity	2 Detached
3 Group	3 Focused
4 Multi-style	4 Singleness
5 Burlesque	5 Silence
6 Timeless	6 Shaping
7 Self-controlled	7 Structure
8 Projective	8 Constructing
9 Outer-stimulated	9 Abstract
10 Theatre of the physical	10 Contained

Figure A.2 Lists of constructs (10 for each dramatherapist)

1. Choose 12 elements. Write these down in any order.

2. Take the first three of your list. What do two of them have in contrast to the third? Write this down in the space above the first rank. This is the first construct (a).

3. Beginning at your second element, take the next three on the list, and discover what two of them have in common, apart from the third. This is your second construct. Insert in (b).

4. Continue until all your constructs have been inserted.

5. Write down your elements in the order in which you have been using them, in the element column.

6. Using a scale of 1–7 (central point 4, highest point 1), rank each element in respect of each construct.

CONSTRUCTS

		a *Symbolic*[1]	b	c	d	e	f	g	h	i	j
	1	*Fantasy journey*[2]									
	2										
E	3										
L	4										
E	5										
M	6										
E	7										
N	8										
T	9										
S	10										
	11										
	12										

1 Example construct

2 Example element

Figure A.3 Instruction sheet for grid test

6. The rank order grid permits several forms of analysis, both by hand and computer methods. In this case, rank order correlations were run by hand between each pair of rankings. The two constructs accounting for most of the variance (i.e. correlating most highly with other constructs) were used to form the axes of a simple graph (Figure A.4). (The second axis is the one that accounts for most of the common variance once the first has been taken out, without being statistically dependent on it. 'Relationship scores' have been arrived at by squaring the original rank order correlations and multiplying by 100.) Graphs which show particularly high correlation of constructs are 1, 4, 7, 9, 10; however, most graphs reveal a higher degree of interest and involvement within the areas of imagination and personal relationship than anything else.

7. A list of constructs considered to have spiritual significance or implications accounted for 44.6 per cent of the total variance (Figures A.5 and A.6). These constructs made up 44.5 per cent of the total number of constructs. This list represents an attempt to distinguish those constructs which might be considered implicitly religious from those that did not appear to suggest religion in any way. Constructs were included if they implied: (a) the relationship between and among persons, love and understanding; (b) morality and personal responsibility; (c) the use of imagery to express awareness of what is reached out for but not grasped;[1] (d) a sense of human destiny and purpose; the transcendence of present experience. When these constructs had been identified, it was found that the mean of their individual relationship scores was almost exactly the same as that of the remainder of the constructs (4.08 as opposed to 4.13)[2] There were 49 selected 'religious' constructs out of a total of 110 constructs. These 49 accounted for roughly as much as the total variance – i.e. their importance in relating to other constructs as the other 61 did. In other words, there were almost as many 'religious' factors in the dramatherapists' ways of looking at dramatherapy as there were factors of other kinds; and they were structurally more important in contributing to the way that the individuals in the group organised their awareness, including as they did attitudes, ideas and experiences of considerable importance for their own personal interpretation of life.

---

1 The group of objects representing metaphor and symbol–metaphor, projection, symbolic story, symbolic play, archetypes, symbolic use of media, objects and toy animals – 14 constructs, (including repeats) amounting to 12.7 per cent of the total number, made up for 27.5 per cent of the variance of the 'religious' group.

2 t = 0.176 (with 109 d.f. t = 1.980 at the 0.05 level of significance).

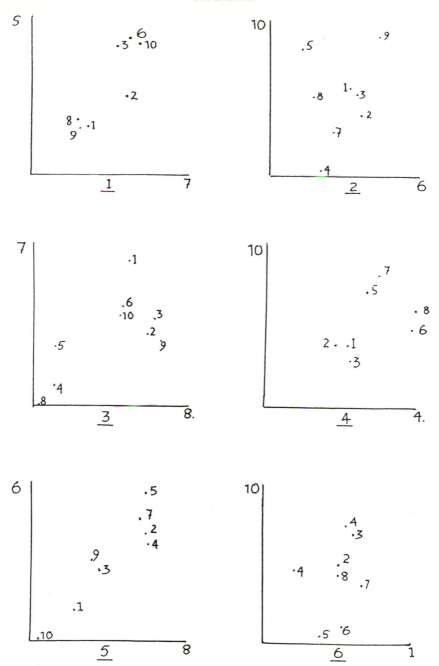

Note: Underlined figures refer to individual construct graphs; figures at the corners of graphs refer to dominant constructs in each graph

Figure A.4. Graphs showing individual dramatherapists' ordering of their own constructs

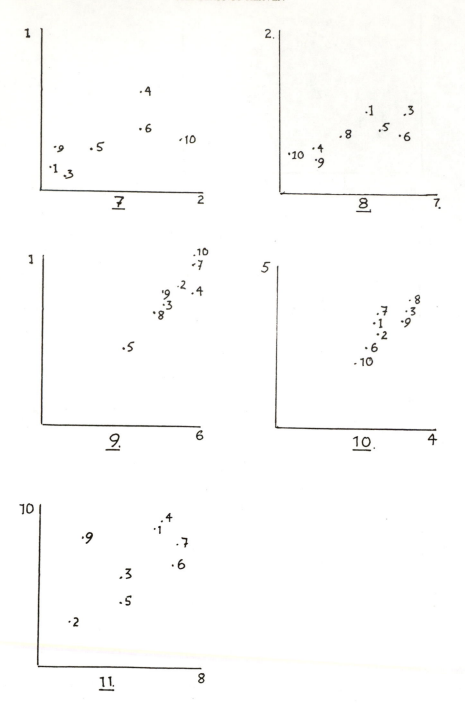

Figure A.4. (continued)

SURPRISE[A]   Fantasy[A] (0.89), Imagination[A] (0.92),
                                    Projective play[A] (0.87)

CREATIVE   Echoing[D] (0.87), Spontaneity[A] (0.93)

WISH-FULFILMENT[A]   Fantasy[A] (0.92), Embodiment (0.93)

INTRAPERSONAL[B]   Interpersonal relationships[B] (0.81),
                                    Imaginative space (10.82), Psychological
                                    distance[B] (0.90), Metaphor[A] (0.80)

ACTION   Stimulus (0.81), Humour (0.92),
                                    Relationship[B] (0.88), Movement (0.98)

PRETENDING[A]   Use of fantasy[A] (0.82)

USE OF ROLE[A]   Relationship[B] (0.83), Dramatic[A] (0.86)

BODILY CONSCIOUSNESS   Personal responsibility[C] (0.80), Conflict of
                                    good and evil[C] (0.87), Body/mind
                                    intuition[C] (0.82)

NON-THREATENING   Body (0.80), Narrative[A] (0.87),
                                    Non-verbal (0.87), Imaginative[A] (0.93),
                                    Shape[D] (0.83)

FOCUS[D]   Intensity (0.96), Group (0.88), Multi-style
                                    (0.93), Timeless[A] (0.99), Contrasting with
                                    self[A] (0.98), Projective[A] (0.87),
                                    Outer-stimulated[A] (0.92), Theatre of the
                                    Physical (0.98)

SILENCE   Here (0.84), Singleness[D] (0.86), Sharing[B]
                                    (0.92), Structure[D] (0.94), Contrived[D]
                                    (0.89).

    A = Implying transcendence or beyondness
    B = Implying encounter or relationship
    C = Implying good or evil
    D = Implying shape, definition, meaning

Figure A.5.

		Variance score
Empathic insight (4)		1649
Individual focus, personal (3)		775
Significant other		187
Relationship, *inter*personal (3)		1102
*Intra*personal		558
Good and evil		346
Universality		371
Personal responsibility/insight (2)		679
Timeless		729
Child-like		203
Magic		505
Imagination and fantasy (6)		2583
Embodiment (4)		1815
Narrative, story (2)		874
Epic		420
Journey		409
Intensity		703
Imaginative space		521
Symbol and metaphor (includes archetypes and unconscious symbols; symbolic use of a medium; projective use of objects, symbolic stories (14)		5408.6
	49 constructs	19,837.6
Total variance	110 constructs	44,450

Figure A.6. Constructs having a degree of religious significance

8. A different construct played the dominant role (i.e. accounted for most of the variance) in the way that each dramatherapist construed the elements of dramatherapy that were supplied. The constructs were: surprise, creative, wish-fulfilment, interpersonal action, pretending, use of role, bodily consciousness, non-threatening, focus, and constructing. These constructs thus represent important factors in the way that these individuals think and feel about dramatherapy; their thinking tends in the direction of these ideas, and they *judge matters to do with dramatherapy in terms of these constructs.*

It will be seen that none of them is explicitly religious. On the other hand, some of these constructs are highly correlated with constructs that have a religious tone or reference, or which are often considered to be components of religious awareness. A list of constructs highly correlated with the core constructs of each grid is given in Figure A.5. The ones which appear to me to have religious implications are marked A, B, C and D:

A, implying transcendence or beyondness;

B, implying encounter or relationship;

C, implying good or evil;

D, implying shape, definition, meaning.

There are 17 As, 7 Bs, 3 Cs and 6 Ds, 33 out of 51 highly related constructs (65%.)

The criteria for implicit religiousness are of course open to question. 'Wish-fulfilment', for example, is included, but 'Magic' is not, seeming to signify a directly instrumental relationship with the unseen. 'Dramatic' is in, because of the implication of betweenness and beyondness which it has in the grid; but 'Creative' is out because in this instance it was explicitly limited to human creativity. Constructs of 'Embodiment' might in this context be considered to be implicitly religious, as the body is regarded within dramatherapy as the symbol or icon of personhood. The idea that human flesh is implicitly religious is itself explicitly religious according to the terms of at least one religion. In an investigation like this it is difficult, if not impossible, to avoid 'experimenter bias'. This may seem an over-subjective choice of constructs. Readers are invited to draw their own conclusions as to whether or not any of these constructs, or construct clusters, can be taken as being 'implicitly religious'. Obviously, the sense in which we mean things can be seen by the things we associate with them; no construct cluster reveals explicit religiosity, but several clusters show the association of ideas connected with spiritual awareness.

Summary

Whilst telling us little about the relationship between explicit religion and dramatherapy, the results show the significance of factors in dramatherapists' understanding of their treatment modality which are normally associated with spiritual awareness and religious belief. In particular, constructs connected with symbolism play a definitive part in the overall picture. Of the two this would seem to be the more important finding, because of the centrality of symbolism to religion, and the fact that the other one depends largely on my own opinion as to whether or not a particular construct can be validly regarded as in some way religious. Two of the constructs making up the symbolism 'package' suggest explicit religion, although in one of its less common forms, i.e. 'unconscious symbolism' and 'archetypes'. At the same time it should be remembered that in this case no questions about religion or spirituality were asked.

'Laddering' of Thirteen Dramatherapists

A second group of dramatherapists were subjected to the diagnostic process that construct psychologists call 'laddering'. This consists of asking why somebody construes a particular element in a particular way, and going on to question the answers they give in order to reach a fundamental value or reason, one which the person considers to be self-evident. Laddering is a way of arriving at 'super-ordinate constructs', in other words, those exerting most influence on our ways of understanding and validating the things with which we come into contact.

I put the following question to the dramatherapists: 'What is the most important thing, for you, about dramatherapy?' I asked them to answer as quickly as they could, by saying the first thing they thought of that distinguished dramatherapy from other therapeutic approaches. Answers were written down in construct form, i.e. the thing plus its opposite. Having received the answer I enquired as to what it was about the chosen construct that the person considered to be particularly important. (Sometimes I just said 'Why?') This went on until he or she arrived at a construct that seemed to express a fundamental evaluation, representing the basic, irreducible reason why dramatherapy was important for them. The results are given in Figure A.7.

The thirteen superordinate constructs pertaining to dramatherapy elicited by the laddering approach were: clarity–obscurity; desperation–serenity; release–captivity/stuckness; people–things; meaning/purpose–meaninglessness/purposelessness; individual–merging; person–types/categories; sharing–demanding; life–death; interpersonal–intrapersonal; healing–atrophying; health–illness; life–death (psychological). These constructs represent a final evaluative measure. For these people, dramatherapy is essentially either more or less clear, serene, a release, concerned with people, meaningful, concerned with individuals, personal, sharing, concerned with life, interpersonal, healing, concerned with health (which is another way of saying obscure, desperate, concerned with captivity, thing-like, meaningless, merging, to do with types, demanding, concerned with death, intrapersonal, atrophying, concerned with illness).

This should leave us in no doubt of the seriousness with which dramatherapists regard their discipline. All drama concerns the difference between things and people, meaning and meaninglessness, serenity and desperation, healing and atrophying, life and death (which occurred twice). Several people drew attention to personality factors, and the crucial importance of the relationship of self and other. These do not denote any specifically (doctrinally) religious awareness; but they certainly reveal a fundamental commitment to values held to be ultimate.

The original answer to the question 'What is the most important thing for you about dramatherapy?' is given on the left, with the opposing pole of the construct on the right. The sloping lines indicate the pole followed up by the questioner. The connections are those made by the Subject.

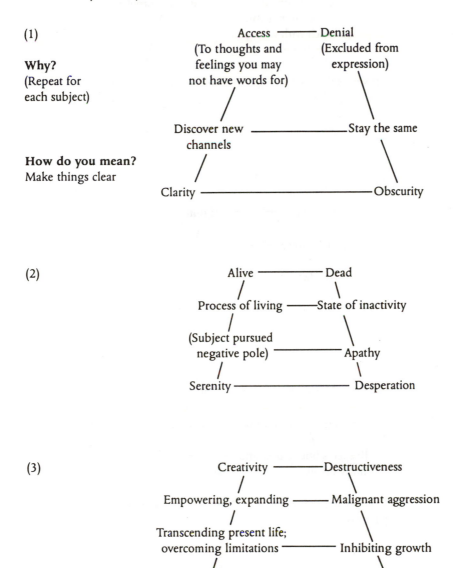

(1)

Why?
(Repeat for
each subject)

Access ——— Denial
(To thoughts and   (Excluded from
feelings you may   expression)
not have words for)

Discover new ——————— Stay the same
channels

How do you mean?
Make things clear

Clarity ———————————— Obscurity

(2)

Alive ——— Dead

Process of living ——— State of inactivity

(Subject pursued ——— Apathy
negative pole)

Serenity ——————— Desperation

(3)

Creativity ——— Destructiveness

Empowering, expanding ——— Malignant aggression

Transcending present life;
overcoming limitations ——— Inhibiting growth

Catharsis/release ——————— Captivity/stuckness

Figure A.7. Laddering

(4)

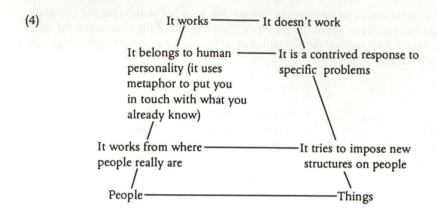

(5)

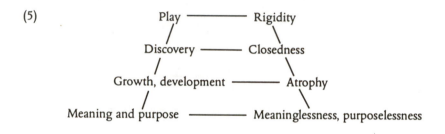

(6)

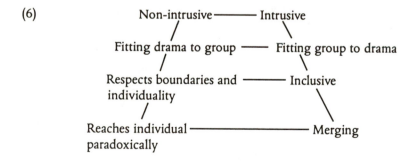

Figure A.7 (continued)

(7)

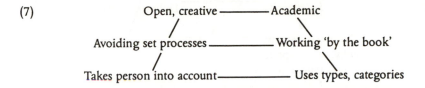

Open, creative ——————— Academic

Avoiding set processes ——————— Working 'by the book'

Takes person into account——————— Uses types, categories

(8)

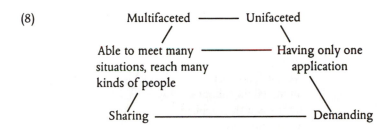

Multifaceted ——————— Unifaceted

Able to meet many ——————— Having only one
situations, reach many   application
kinds of people

Sharing ——————————————— Demanding

(9)

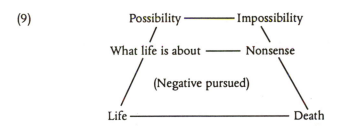

Possibility ——————— Impossibility

What life is about ——— Nonsense

(Negative pursued)

Life ——————————————— Death

(10)

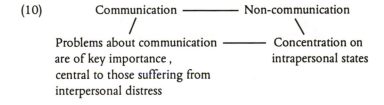

Communication ——————— Non-communication

Problems about communication ——————— Concentration on
are of key importance ,   intrapersonal states
central to those suffering from
interpersonal distress

Figure A.7 (continued)

(11)

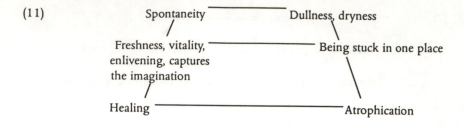

(12)

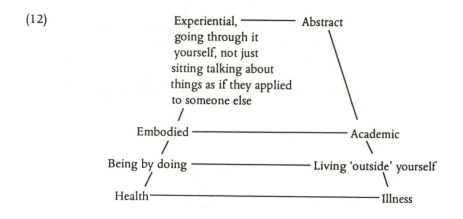

(13)

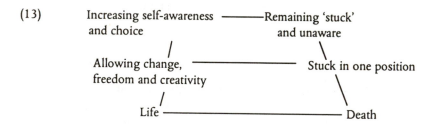

Figure A.7 (continued)

Message and Meta-message in Dramatherapy

Gregory Bateson points out how very important this distinction is for the purpose of psychotherapy. The therapist has always to know what is story, and what 'story about story'; or as Bateson distinguishes them, 'message' and 'meta-message'. The interplay of message and meta-message is the mode of normal human communication. Without the distinction between message (what I say) and meta-message (how I say it), no fully human communication can take place. We are constantly signalling information about what kind of message our message is. The secret is an open one. Most of the time there is no attempt to deceive. We need to be free to use the uniquely human technique of being able to comment on our own message, modulating its impact in ways that we alone decide. A host of personal media – gesture, tone of voice, choice of phraseology or idiom, facial expression, bodily posture, position in space, manipulation of idea and context – tell people how we want what we are saying to be understood. Drama makes this interchange obvious. To this extent it works to clarify confusion. Standing back from what is being presented to us, we are in a position to identify the means of presentation and take this into account. A play is the very clearest demonstration of the ways in which the logic of communication-types affects the interplay between modes of personal reality.

Confusion between message and meta-message is always misleading and may be deeply disturbing. Bateson suggested that people suffering from schizophrenia 'have trouble in identifying and interpreting those signals which should tell the individual what sort of a message a message is, i.e. trouble with signals of the same logical type as "this is a play"' (1973: 167f). Difficulties arise when message and meta-message get confused; 'things' and 'kinds of thing' do not belong to the same 'logical type', and when they are treated as if they did, it can be hard to make sense of the world. An example of this is the use of metaphor, which is a way of classifying things and people along imaginary lines – using the imagination to describe what kind of person or thing we are considering. Usually we are quite clear what is to be recognised as itself and what has to be looked at in another way in terms of something else. I do not change the actual existence of the pile of books on the table when I call them 'a mountain of second-hand paperbacks', although calling them this allows me to assume a particular relationship to them.

Schizoid people tend to confuse metaphor with literal description. Everything fits together in the same kind of way, metaphor being taken literally and simple statement being given a meta-logical significance. The paradigm human situation for this is that of the unfortunate mother who, because her rejection of her child is unacceptable to her and everybody else, deliberately obscures the nature of her communication with him or her. As a result, 'the child is punished for discriminating accurately what she is expressing, and he or she is punished for discriminating inaccurately' (Bateson, 1973: 186). Such a child is caught in a trap from which she or he cannot possibly escape by using ordinary human logic, which depends on discerning similarities, namely the non- or supra-logical relationship between message and meta-message. The verbal message is precise, but the background one has all the primitive force of pre-verbal primary process communication. The child is caught in a trap, punished both for 'seeing through' mother to the cruel truth of her underlying hostility, and for drawing close in obedience to her protestations of love, thus activating her hostility. Bateson says 'The double-bind may be summarised as an experience of being punished precisely for being right in one's view of the context' (1973: 206).

Such a person may grow up with no way of knowing what kind of communication any particular message is; indeed, for him or her there is only one kind of communication, and this rules out the possibility of using one kind to stand for another, as in analogy, metaphor, drama, slang, etc. Normally, human communication is two-dimensional: 'What I say' and, at the same time but on another level, 'what the way I'm saying it says'. The second admits me to the real meaning and significance of the first; the real person who is speaking to me. Bateson's claim is that, if this kind of real communication has been powerful and unwelcome, I prefer to stay on the surface...

It is this fear of contextual meaning that leads to the dread of intimacy in personal relationships that characterises schizophrenia. If 'second level' communication has become too confusing or too threatening in its significance it may be avoided, and the project whereby we know and are known *in depth* as we exchange background information about the meaning of our meanings, finally abandoned. With it goes all possibility of genuine relationship, because that always involves telling the other how our communications are to be interpreted. In other words, letting him or her *in*. It has always been recognised that any consideration of dramatherapy as a means of treating psychological illness must take account of its nature as a way of manipulating an individual's experience of other people, and involve experimenting with relationship.

As we have seen, relationship depends upon mystery. To understand at the explicit level of the message's stated content while ignoring its hidden dimensions is to assert an inauthentic continuity with the other which amounts to a cognitive take-over. Relationship is subtler and more profound. It concerns distance from and involvement with other people. The second factor is more obvious than the first, but it is on the first that the second depends. We must be able to stand back and observe before we can move forward and embrace, or let ourselves be embraced. The best known expression of this principle is in Martin Buber's *I and*

Thou. Buber imagines two human 'worlds', that of 'I' and that of 'It', the first of which is the sphere of involvement with experience, the second the sphere of drawing conclusions from experience. According to the nature of human consciousness the two worlds continually interact, each contributing to the life of the other: '"It" the eternal chrysalis, "Thou" the eternal butterfly.' There can be no life that is authentically human which does not depend on the alternation of 'Thou' and 'It' (1966).

It has been suggested that depression involves the kind of experience that exaggerates involvement at the expense of detachment, 'Thou' at the expense of 'It'. In contrast, schizoid states are associated with too little contact, 'It' dominating 'Thou', and preventing a healthy balance between the two. Elsewhere, I have used a personal construct approach to describe the tendency of depressed and schizophrenic people to 'stay in one position' with regard to their experience of themselves and other people. Depressed people feel themselves condemned to a limited range of ways of behaving, none of which affords an escape from the demands incurred by the situation in which they are emotionally and intellectually enmeshed. Involvement (the 'Thou') has hold of them and they cannot move, cannot assert themselves and be free.

> Because the number of available constructs about the self is limited, it is less possible to 'think round' the self-punitive attitude of mind (the attitude induced by taking the role supplied or imposed by punitive others) that sees itself as confined to the negative pole of all available ways of looking at life. (Grainger, 1990: 41)

Schizoid awareness, on the other hand, subsists in the tendency to construe life according to the impersonal 'It' mode. This is equally hard to relinquish, if not more so, not because it offers too much scope for involvement but because it provides too little. Our relationship with people is the key to our world. They are the structural elements around which perception is ordered. Things by themselves are not enough to make it all hang together. Many psychologists and psychiatrists have drawn attention to the problems that arise when those cast by circumstance in highly significant roles in a child's personal drama either refuse, or are unable, to order their actions clearly enough to create a consistent family structure, to communicate clear messages that do not cancel themselves out.

In our most important encounters, semantic clarity is essential for the establishment of an ordered and self-consistent personal universe. Important meanings which are systematically confused undermine the everyday fabric of recognisable sense. If they are actually self-contradictory they may lead to distrust of ordinary communication because they cannot be relied upon as ways of judging intentions and predicting events. They give rise to the idea that 'What happens does not seem to have any bearing on what people say, so there is no point in my trying to get through to anybody about anything.' If relationship, which depends on communication, is the key to human wholeness, the break-down of communication is bound to have a disastrous effect. We can imagine the confused person saying something like this to him or herself: 'If I depend on what they say I lay myself open to perpetual disappointment, because, whatever happens I always seem to get it wrong. My own private world is more to be preferred, because I can make my own rules and trust my own interpretations.' Unfortunately it is the process of receiving validation for the responses we make to our personal situation that makes these responses practical ways of living in the world; and the only validation which really counts comes from outside. That is, it is given to us by *other people.*

Those who order their interior worlds in this exclusive way find that their thinking becomes more and more disordered. If they are not able to 'be themselves' in public, they will develop an alternative self in private. Seeing that the self is defined in terms of its messages to the other, private selves must pay a harsh price for their exclusiveness. 'Schizophrenic thought-disorder is experienced subjectively as living in a fluid unfocussed and undifferentiated world in which anxiety is not felt to any marked degree since only the vaguest and least destructible anticipations arise in the mind of the subject' (Bannister, 1962: 841).

For depressed people, dramatherapy is a reminder that they live in a world in which men and women are free agents, able to make valid personal decisions. For schizoid people, it is a reminder that they and others are actually *real:* that they are elements of structure on whom the world depends. These are the 'tight' and 'loose' ways of construing described by Kelly which prevent people from thinking in ways that are flexible and adaptive. One of dramatherapy's main objectives has been that of helping individuals create shareable words – an ambitious project in the case of those in whom 'social communication is crowded out by fantasy' (1955). My own research led me to conclude that dramatherapy provides a valuable degree of structure in situations of emotional and cognitive chaos. In other words, 'The clearly recognizable structure of drama provides an element of shape which counters existential confusion, confusion about personal identity...' 'Dramatherapy, like drama itself, is an arrangement of forms – roles, conventions, contrasts, similarities, modes of understanding, ideas and feelings – which encourages us to discriminate between and choose among a range of different kinds of perception or ways of perceiving' (1990: 11). In it, people whose ways of construing reality are too inflexible, or too uncertain, to allow them to articulate a personal universe capable of providing the foundations for realistic action upon the world while remaining open to change by the world, identify with ways of being that reflect a more balanced humanity, one which draws nearer to achieving the natural reciprocity of I and Thou.

As we have seen, lack of distance between self and other characterises both depression and schizophrenia. There is a tendency for personal reality to be 'cut down to size' for easier assimilation. People become thing-like, insomuch as they lose their dimension of autonomous life, the characteristic that distinguishes them from objects. Dramatherapy is concerned to draw the lines which separate the setting from the characters taking part in the action as clearly as possible. It is designed to show where people end and ideas begin. These are real people; they cannot be thought away or ignored. What they are doing is real, too, even though it has been invented. Above all, dramatherapy is unavoidably three-dimensional, communicating in depth. It uses a simple but effective paradigm to demonstrate message and meta-message that of aesthetic distance, showing us how we stand in relation to what is over against us.

Bibliography

Bailey, E. (1989) *Implicit Perception of God*. Winterbourne: Network for the Study of Implicit Regligion.

Bannister, D. (1962) 'The Nature and Measurement of Schizophrenic Thought Disorder'. *Journal of Mental Science 108*, 824–842.

Bateson, G. (1973) *Steps Towards an Ecology of Mind*. St. Albans: Paladin.

Bowlby, J. (1981) *Attachment and Loss* Vols. 1–3. London: Penguin.

Buber, M. (1957) *Pointing the Way*. London: Routledge.

Buber, M. (1961) *Between Man and Man*. London: Collins.

Buber, M. (1962) *Werke* Vol. 1. Munich and Heidelberg: Kösel-Verlag and Verlag Lambert Schneider.

Buber, M. (1966) *I and Thou*. Edinburgh: T. & T. Clark.

Burns, G. (1972) *Theatricality: A Study of Conventionality in Theatre and Social Life*. New York: Harper and Row.

Butcher, S.H. (ed) (1951) *Aristotle's Theory of Poetry and Fine Art*. New York: Dover.

Campbell, J. (1988) *The Hero with a Thousand Faces*. London: Paladin.

Casson, J. (1978) 'Shamanistic Elements of Oriental Theatre, with Special Reference to The Traditional Forms of Drama in Sri Lanka', Birmingham, Birmingham University MA Thesis (unpub.).

Casson, J. (1984) 'The Therapeutic Dramatic Community Ceremonies of Sri Lanka'. *Journal of British Association for Dramatherapists 7*, 2, 11–18.

Casson, J. (1989) 'Notes on Dramatherapy with Schizophrenic Patients' (unpub.).

Chamisso, A. (1957) *Peter Schlemihl*, London: Calder and Boyars.

Douglas, M. (1966) *Purity and Danger*. London: Routledge.

Einstein, A. (1935) *The World As I See It*. London: Lane

Elam, K. (1988) *Semiotics of Theatre and Drama*. London: Routledge.

Eliade, M. (1958) *Patterns in Comparative Religion*. London: Sheed and Ward.

Eliade, M. (1959) *The Sacred and the Profane*. San Diego: Harcourt Brace.

Eliade, M. (1965) *Rites and Symbols of Initiation*. New York: Harper and Row.

Eliade, M. (1968) *Myths, Dreams and Mysteries*. London: Collins.

Eliade, M. (1970) *Shamanism: Archaic Techniques of Ecatasy*. Princeton: Princeton University Press.

Elkin, A.P. (1946) *Aboriginal Man of High Degree*. Sydney: Sydney University Press.

'Endo, T. *see* Toshikatsu Endo'

Ferenzi, S. (1950) *Further Contributions to the Theory and Technique of Psychoanalysis*. London: Institute of Psychoanalysis.

Flowers, J.V. (1975) 'Simulation and Role Playing Methods'. In F.M. Kanfer and A.P. Goldstein (eds) *Helping People Change*. London: Pergamon.

Frankl, V.E. (1973) *Psychotherapy and Existentialism*. London: Penguin.

Frankl, V.E. (1975) *The Unconscious God*. London: Hodder and Stoughton.

Freud, S. (1949) *An Outline of Psychoanalysis*. London: Hogarth Press.

Frye, N. (1957) *Anatomy of Criticism*. Princeton: Princeton University Press.

Geertz, C. (1968) 'Religion as a Cultural System'. In M. Banton (ed) *Anthropological Approaches to the Study of Religion*. London: Tavistock.

Gennep, A. Van (1960) *The Rites of Passage*. (trans. M.B.Vizedom and C.L.Caffee), London: Routledge.

Gersie, A. (1990) *Storymaking in Education and Therapy*. London: Jessica Kingsley Publishers.

Gordon, R. (1983) 'The Creative Process: Self Expression and Self Transcendence'. In S. Jennings (ed) *Creative Therapy*. Banbury: Kemble Press.

Gorman, C. (1972) *The Book of Ceremony*. Cambridge: Whole Earth Tools.

Grainger, R. (1974) *The Language of the Rite*. London: Darton, Longman and Todd.

Grainger, R. (1985) 'Using Drama Creatively in Therapy'. *Dramatherapy 8*, 2.

Grainger, R. (1987) *Staging Posts*. Braunton: Merlin.

Grainger, R. (1988a) *The Unburied*. Worthing: Churchman Publ.

Grainger, R. (1988b) *The Message of the Rite*. Cambridge: Lutterworth.

Grainger, R. (1990) *Drama and Healing*. London; Jessica Kingsley Publishers.

Halmos, P. (1965) *The Faith of the Counsellors*. London: Constable.

Hameline, J.-Y. (1972) 'Les Rites de Passage'. *La Maison Dieu 112* (Spring), 133–143 (Paris).

Hertzberg, A. (ed) (1968) *Out of the Whirlwind*. New York: Union of American Hebrew Congregations.

Hillman, J. (1979) *The Dream and the Underworld*. New York: Harper and Row.

Hillman, J. (1983) *Healing Fiction*. New York: Station Hill.

Jacobi, J. (1962) *The Psychology of C.G. Jung*. London: Routledge.

Jennings, S. (ed) (1983) *Creative Therapy*. Banbury: Kemble Press.

Jennings, S. (1983) 'Models of Practice in Dramatherapy', *Dramatherapy 7*, 1.

Jennings, S. (ed) (1987) *Dramatherapy: Theory and Practice for Teachers and Clinicians* Vol. 1. London: Croom Helm.

Jennings, S. (1990) *Dramatherapy with Families, Groups and Individuals: Waiting in the Wings*. London: Jessica Kingsley Publishers.

Jennings, S. (1995) *Theatre, Ritual and Transformation*. London: Routledge.

Johnson, D.R. (1981) 'Some Diagnostic Implications of Dramatherapy'. In G. Schattner and R. Courtney. *Drama in Therapy* Vol. 2. New York: Drama Book Specialists.

Jung, C.G. (1940) *The Integration of the Personality*. London: Kegan Paul.

Jung, C.G. (1959) 'Archetypes and the Collective Unconscious'. *Collected Works* Vol. 9. London: Routledge and Kegan Paul.

Jung, C.G. (1976) *Modern Man In Search of a Soul*. London: Routledge.

Jung, C.G. (1977) *Memories, Dreams and Reflections*. London: Collins.

Jung, C.G. (1983) *Psychology and Religion*. New Haven, CT: Yale University Press.

Kelly, G.A. (1955) *The Psychology of Personal Constructs*. New York: Norton.

Kelly, G.A. (1963) *A Theory of Personality*. New York: Norton.

Kempe, A.B. (1890) 'On the Relation Between the Logical Theory of Classes and the Geometrical Theory of Points'. *Proceedings of the London Mathematical Society 21*.

Kilburn, B. and Richardson, J.T. (1984) 'Psychology and New Religions in a Pluralistic Society'. *American Psychologist 39*, 3.

Kirby, E.T. (1975) *Ur-Drama*. New York University Press.

Koltai, J. (1981) 'Movement, Drama and Therapy', In G. Schattner and R. Courtney. *Drama in Therapy* Vol. 2. New York: Drama Book Specialists.

Landy, R. (1986) *Drama Therapy: Concepts and Practice*. Springfield: Thomas.

Langley, D. (1983) *Dramatherapy and Psychiatry*. London: Croom Helm.

Lewis, I.M. (1971) *Ecstatic Religion*. London: Penguin.

Lorenz, K. (1967) *On Aggression*. New York: Bantam.

Lukes, S. (1975) *Emile Durkheim*. London: Penguin.

Masson, J. (1978) 'The Noble Path of Buddhism'. In W. Foy (ed) *Man's Religious Quest*. London: Croom Helm.

May, R. (1975) *The Courage To Create*. London: Collins.

McNiff, S. (1988) 'The Shaman Within', *The Arts in Therapy 15*, 4.

McGuire, W. and Hull, R.F.C. (1978) *C.G. Jung Speaking*. London: Thames and Hudson.

Mead, G.H. (1967) *Mind, Self and Society*. Chicago: Chicago University Press.

Moreno, J.J. (1988) 'The Music Therapist: Creative Arts Therapist and Contemporary Shaman', in *The Arts in Psychotherapy 15*, 4.

Moreno, J.L. (1946) *Psychodrama 1*, NY: Beacon House.

Moreno, J.L (1947) *The Theatre of Spontaneity*. New York: Beacon House.

Moreno, J.L (1959) *Psychodrama 2*. (with Z. T. Moreno). New York: Beacon House.

Ofshe, R., Berg, W.E., Coughlin, R., Dolinajee, G., Gerson, K. and Johnson, A. (1974) 'Social Structure and Social Control in Syanon'. *Journal of Voluntary Action Research 3*.

Pepper, S. (1942) *World Hypotheses*. Berkeley, University of California Press.

Pernoud, R. (1973) *Heloise and Abelard*. London: Collins.

Read, K. (1965) *The High Valley*. New York: Scribner's.

Reason, P. and Rowan, J. (1981) *Human Enquiry: A Source Book of New Paradigm Research*. Chichester: Wiley.

Rees, E. (1992) *Christian Symbols, Ancient Roots*. London: Jessica Kingsley Publishers.

Sarbin, T.E. (1986) *Narrative Psychology*. New York: Praeger.

Schäbe, K.E. (1986) 'Self Narrative and Adventure'. In T.E. Sarbin (ed) *Narrative Psychology*. New York: Praeger.

Schattner, G. and Courtney, R. (eds) (1981) *Drama in Therapy*. New York: Drama Book Specialists, (Vols. 1 and 2).

Schechner, R. (1988) *Performance Theory*. London: Routledge.

Scheff, T.J. (1980) *Catharsis in Drama, Healing and Ritual*. Berkley, University of California.

Schmais, C. (1988) 'Creative Arts Therapies and Shamanism: A Comparison', *The Arts in Psychotherapy 15*, 4.

Simmel, G. (1950) *The Sociology of Georg Simmel* (ed and trans Kurt Wolff). Glencoe, IL: Free Press.

Sivaraman, K. (1974) 'The Meaning of Moksha in Contemporary Hindu Thought'. In S.J. Samartha (ed) *Living Faiths and Ultimate Gods*. Geneva, World Council of Churches.

Slade, P. (1981) 'Dramatherapy'. In G. Schattner and R. Courtney (eds) *Drama in Therapy*, Vol. 2, New York: Drama Book Specialists.

Sussman, L. (1984) 'Creating Personal Myth'. New York: Union Graduate School PhD Thesis (unpub.)

Suttie, I.D. (1988) *The Origins of Love and Hate*. London: Free Association Books.

Toshikatsu Endo (1992) Exhibition Programme, Yorkshire Sculpture Park, Wakefield.

Turner, B.S. (1991) *Religion and Social Theory*. London: Sage.

Turner, V. (1985) *On the Edge of the Bush*. Tucson: University of Arizona Press.

Williams, C. (1937) *Descent into Hell*. London: Faber.

Wilshire, B. (1982) *Role-Playing and Identity*. Bloomington: Indiana University Press.

Winnicott, D.W. (1971) *Playing and Reality*. London: Tavistock.

Yinger, O.M. (1970) *The Scientific Study of Religion*. New York: Macmillan.

Subject Index

Author Index

Jung, C. 31–2, 49, 87

Kelly, G.A. 7, 55, 79, 90, 110, 128
Kempe, A.B. 62
Kilburn, B. 59
Kirby, E.T. 34
Koltai, J. 11

Bannister, D. 128
Bailey, E. 100
Bateson, G. 125, 126
Bowlby, J. 17
Buber, M. 2, 22, 23, 24, 25, 29, 86, 126–7
Burns, G. 56
Butcher, S.H. 23

Campbell, J. 69
Casson, J. 10, 24, 30, 31, 32, 34, 38–9, 43, 44
Chamisso, A. 78

Douglas, M. 55

Einstein, A. 46–7
Elam, K. 56
Eliade, M. See Toshikatsu Endo
Elkin, A.P. 58
Endo, T. 22

Ferenzi, S. 18
Flowers, J.V. 56
Frankl, V. 45
Freud, S. 2, 18
Frye, N. 57, 77, 78, 88

Geertz, C. 108
Gennep, A. Van 9, 29
Gersie, A. 7, 45, 46
Gordon, R. 11
Grainger, R. 7, 11, 25, 49, 56, 59, 62, 69, 70, 98, 127, 128

Hadfield, J. 17
Halmos, P. 1, 18
Hameline, J.-Y. 62
Hertzberg, A. 15
Hillman, J. 80
Hull, R.F.C. 87

Jennings, S. 6–7, 7, 9, 60, 61, 63, 89
Johnson, D.R. 10, 24

Landy, R. 6
Langley, D. 9, 66
Langley, G. 10
Lewis, I.M. 38
Lorenz, K. 32–3
Lukes, S. 89

Masson, J. 16
May, R. 11
McGuire, W. 87
McNiff, S. 39, 43
Mead, G.H. 7
Moreno, J. 7, 35, 39, 43

Ofshe, R. 60

Pepper, S. 68, 85, 107
Pernoud, R. 25–6

Read, K. 34
Reason, P. 8
Rees, E. 108
Richardson, J.T. 59
Rowan, J. 8

Schäbe, K.E. 78
Schechner, R. 30, 32, 33, 34, 36, 102–3
Scheff, T.J. 6
Schmais, C. 43
Simmel, G. 100
Sivaraman, K. 16
Slade, P. 10
Sussman, L. 45
Suttie, I.D. 17, 18, 35

Toshikatsu Endo 22

Turner, B.S. 101
Turner, V. 104

Williams, C. 24
Wilshire, B. 6
Winnicott, D.W. 7

Yinger, O.M. 98